# SMALLVILLE

## SEASON 7

### THE OFFICIAL COMPANION

Superman created by Jerry Siegel and Joe Shuster

SMALLVILLE: THE OFFICIAL COMPANION SEASON 7
ISBN: 9781845767150

Published by
Titan Books
A division of
Titan Publishing Group Ltd
144 Southwark St
London
SE1 0UP

First edition October 2008
10 9 8 7 6 5 4 3 2 1

Visit our websites:
**www.titanbooks.com**
**www.dccomics.com**

Did you enjoy this book? We love to hear from our readers. Please
email us at **readerfeedback@titanemail.com** or write to us at
Reader Feedback at the above address.

To receive advance information, news, competitions, and exclusive Titan
offers online, please register as a member by clicking the "sign up"
button on our website: www.titanbooks.com

A CIP catalogue record for this title is available from the British Library.

Printed and bound in the United States.

# SMALLVILLE
## SEASON 7
### THE OFFICIAL COMPANION

Craig Byrne

TITAN BOOKS

## ACKNOWLEDGMENTS

Thanks go out to Cath Trechman and Adam Newell at Titan for the opportunity to work on my fourth *Smallville* companion book; Susan Kesser, Kendra Voth, Neil Sadhu, and the managers, publicists, and assistants who made several of these interviews happen; Mark, Bryan, Jesse, Derek @ SHoE, Jason, Brian, Cheryl, Tabitha, Heather, Rebecca, Tamela, Nate, Jayme, Jake, Melanie, Triplet, and others who showed support as I was working on this book; and Chris Cerasi and Steve Korté at DC Comics.

Special thanks go out to Alfred Gough and Miles Millar for creating *Smallville* in the first place; to Michael Rosenbaum, John Glover, Laura Vandervoort, and Kristin Kreuk, whose regular presence on the show will be missed; and to the fans at KryptonSite, who have encouraged my meteor habit for seven years now.

The writer would also like to express gratitude to the cast and crew members from *Smallville* who gave their time to be interviewed and/or have shared some of their behind-the-scenes photographs for this book: Al Gough, Miles Millar, Todd Slavkin, Darren Swimmer, Brian Peterson, Kelly Souders, Michael Rosenbaum, Allison Mack, Erica Durance, Aaron Ashmore, Laura Vandervoort, John Glover, James Marsters, Justin Hartley, Alaina Huffman, Helen Slater, Christopher Heyerdahl, Michael Cassidy, Phil Morris, Anna Galvin, Mike Walls, John Wash, Aleya Naiman, Mairzee Almas, Caroline Cranstoun, James Philpott, Caroline Dries, Al Septien, Turi Meyer, Don Whitehead, Holly Henderson, Holly Harold, John Burke, and Scott Bader. Thanks also go out to the Vancouver crew of *Smallville*, who were very welcoming even as they were rushing to wrap their last pre-strike episode.

— Craig Byrne

The publishers would like to thank the cast and crew of *Smallville* for all their help with this project. Grateful thanks also to Chris Cerasi at DC Comics.

DEDICATION
This book is dedicated to my mother, who has always supported my work and doesn't complain when her vacation is interrupted by my stopping to do book interviews.

# CONTENTS

# FOREWORD BY LAURA VANDERVOORT

Dear *Smallville* Fans,

I can honestly say that this year has brought me so much joy! I had the wonderful, life-altering experience of being cast as Kara Zor-El/Supergirl in the seventh season of *Smallville*. I would never have seen this gift coming, but I'm so grateful that it did.

Thank you for welcoming me into the *Smallville* family and embracing my portrayal of Kara/Supergirl. And, thank you for being the best group of fans I have ever met! You truly do offer the best support and input of any series that I have ever been a part of.

I originally auditioned for the role by videotape from Toronto, as they were casting in LA and I was unavailable to fly out. When I got the call that The CW was interested, I had gotten lost hiking in the woods near my cottage. I eventually found my way back and received several urgent messages on my cell phone asking me to get on a plane as soon as possible to test for the role. I caught an early flight the next morning to LA; when I arrived, I went straight to the screen test.

Once I received the call that I had got the part, I flew home, packed, and then found an

apartment in Vancouver, and a few days later I was wearing Supergirl's classic red and blue and shooting my first scene with Tom Welling!

It was the scene where I open the elevator doors in the *Daily Planet*. *Oh my, he's tall*, I thought when I met Tom. So much was running through my head; I was so nervous to meet the cast!

They all turned out to be great, which was a relief, as joining a cast after they have been a close family for six years can be hard.

Michael Rosenbaum was like no one I have ever met before (in a good way!). He was so funny and so joyful, always making the crew laugh right up to "Action". He and Tom always made me laugh and were such comfortable characters to be around.

I loved the scene in 'Fierce' where Clark tried to teach me to control my power. He used a watermelon in a tutorial on how to control my heat vision. I loved this scene because it was really the first scene where I could relax and be silly. Tom and I laughed and improvized a little. The best

part was when they threw a bucket of watermelon pulp all over him. I tried my best not to laugh during his close up. Ah, the glamor of television!

Erica is also a sweetheart and Allison, Kristin, and Aaron are all wonderful. James Marsters, who plays Brainiac, is such an interesting actor to work with, and challenging for me to work off of. He really is a very layered actor.

Another cool moment for me was working with Helen Slater (the original Supergirl). She is so beautiful and graceful as Lara, Clark's mother. I very much enjoyed our scenes together.

My first experience with flying is one I'll never forget. Who can say they fly for their job — literally *fly*?! My outfits for the first few episodes were somewhat skimpy, so the stunt team had to invent a new harness for me so

it would fit under my tiny costume. I got a few bumps and bruises but loved every minute of it. The show is so well done and so beautifully shot that it was an honor to be a part of it all.

When I wrapped this season, I was sad to see it end. The producers surprised me with my name from the back of my set chair in a beautiful frame. The Props Department also wrapped up something dear to me: Kara's silver cuff from Krypton. It's engraved with the Superman symbol, and I will treasure it forever.

From my first time using heat vision to my first time feeling the agony of kryptonite to my first time flying (which I have on videotape to show my grandchildren one day) I can reflect with you just how much I was able to experience over the course of season seven. I will never forget this time in my acting career.

Thank you to the entire *Smallville* team — the producers, the office staff, and the superb crew and cast. You made my dream a reality.

Love always, your friend and Supergirl,
Laura Dianne Vandervoort

# INTO SEASON SEVEN

CLARK
What the hell are you?

BIZARRO CLARK
I'm you. Only a little more bizarre.

As Clark reacts in puzzled horror, Bizarro Clark charges at him and Clark charges right back. Water sprays from their heels until they

COLLIDE IN SUPERSPEED,

Bizarro's incredible strength sending Clark spinning back into the concrete wall...

EXT. REEVES DAM - DAY

The gigantic edifice looms over the lower reservoir, THE LOUD RUMBLE growing deafening before Clark comes

FLAILING THROUGH THE DAM

right at camera, along with a surging gush of water. As Clark passes, Bizarro Clark follows, soaring at us in a swirling cyclone. As his grinning face FILLS THE FRAME...

SLAM TO BLACK:

"To be continued..."

                    END OF SEASON SIX

## "It's the season of reversals." — Al Gough

In typical *Smallville* fashion, the finale of the sixth season left fans with many unanswered questions. Lana's fate was left up in the air as the van she was driving in exploded, Lex was on the verge of being arrested for her murder, Chloe was at death's door after using her meteor power to save Lois's life, and Clark was confronted by a bio-duplicate Bizarro version of himself. With all these questions left hanging, what would happen in *Smallville* when the seventh season hit our screens?

Fortunately, the show's fandom did not have long to wait! In June 2007, only a few weeks after the screening of the sixth season finale, *TV Guide* broke the news that another Kryptonian would be joining the show — Clark's cousin Kara Zor-El, better known as Supergirl in the comic books. "Kara was sent to Earth in a ship that arrived at the same time as baby Kal-El's," executive producer Al Gough told the magazine. "But there was a problem, and she's been in suspended animation for the last sixteen years. We'll find out in the season première that the big dam break in last season's finale is the reason she's finally awoken." Initially, Kara was described as being enamored with modern Earth culture, loving iPods and popular fashion; however, the more materialistic aspects of her character were toned down by the time she appeared on screen.

Al Gough confirmed their reasons for introducing Kara to the series in The CW's official press release. "One of the joys of creating *Smallville* has been our ability to reinvent and reinterpret classic DC Comics characters," Gough said. "Miles and I believe that Supergirl will give our series the mythic jolt it needs as we head into our seventh season."

Below, left: Chloe and Clark spot danger in the sky.

Below, right: *Lois & Clark*'s Dean Cain as the immortal Dr. Curtis Knox.

Laura Vandervoort's casting as Kara was released in major media publications several weeks later, and in July 2007, Laura joined fellow *Smallville* actors Justin Hartley (Green Arrow), Phil Morris (Martian Manhunter), Erica Durance (Lois Lane), and series creators Al Gough and Miles Millar at Comic-Con International in San Diego. The cast and producers were welcomed with open arms at the convention, where clips from the new season's early episodes were viewed with great enthusiasm. During the convention panel, fans were not only told that Justin Hartley would be returning midseason as the Green Arrow; they were also treated to the exciting news that former Superman Dean Cain would be guest-starring in the fourth episode of season seven as a villainous doctor.

The summer of 2007 brought *Smallville* some well-deserved recognition in the awards arena, with Allison Mack being chosen as the Choice TV Sidekick in the 2007 Teen Choice Awards. *Smallville*'s British Columbia-based crew was also honored for their hard work with several Leo Awards, including Best Dramatic Series.

With announcements about Supergirl, more Green Arrow, Dean Cain, as well as the revelation later that summer that James Marsters would be returning as Brainiac, former *Supergirl* star Helen Slater would be appearing as Clark's Kryptonian mother, Lois Lane would be going after the Luthors, and Clark and Lana would finally get their "real chance", the seventh season of the long-running hit show promised to be an exciting ride... ▪

Above: Clark's Kryptonian cousin added a new dynamic to *Smallville*'s seventh year.

# THE EPISODES

"Hey Clark, have you ever wondered what would happen to all of these humans if you weren't here to play savior? I know you do. You'd just never admit it." — Bizarro

SEASON 7 REGULAR CAST:

**Tom Welling** (Clark Kent)

**Michael Rosenbaum** (Lex Luthor)

**Kristin Kreuk** (Lana Lang)

**Allison Mack** (Chloe Sullivan)

**Erica Durance** (Lois Lane)

**Aaron Ashmore** (Jimmy Olsen)

**Laura Vandervoort** (Kara Zor-El)

**John Glover** (Lionel Luthor)

# BIZARRO

**WRITTEN BY**: Kelly Souders & Brian Peterson
**DIRECTED BY**: Michael Rohl

**GUEST STARS:** Phil Morris (John Jones/The Martian Manhunter), Conrad Coates (Keating), Quinn Lord (Possessed Boy), Jake D. Smith (Boy at Dam), Jacqueline Samuda (Doctor), Suzanne Bastien (Doctor), Randal Edwards (EMT), Anna Galvin (Gina)

**DID YOU KNOW?**

New opening titles premièred with this episode, adding Aaron Ashmore and Laura Vandervoort to the list of series regulars.

The last remaining creature from the Phantom Zone has manifested itself as a bizarre duplicate of Clark. The two titans enter a fierce battle that causes Reeves Dam to rupture. This awakens a long-resting angelic female who saves Lex from a watery doom.

Clark escapes Bizarro long enough to help Lois and Chloe to safety, but for Chloe, it appears to be too late; she is declared legally dead and sent to the morgue. Her apparent death, however, is a temporary side effect of her meteor power, and she awakens on a slab in the morgue very perplexed.

Bizarro suggests to Lex that they form an alliance to kill Clark. Lex pretends to go along with the alien and takes him to the dam before pulling a gun on the duplicate, who promptly knocks Lex out using his superspeed. It's up to the real Clark and the Martian Manhunter, who tricks Bizarro, destroying him by exposing him to Earth's yellow sun.

Although Bizarro is vanquished, Clark continues to suffer the hurt of losing Lana, unaware that she is in fact alive and well on the other side of the world...

## CLARK: They won't always be here. Losing Lana has made me realize no matter how close I get, someday they'll all be gone. And all the time that I've spent ignoring my destiny, trying to be something I'll never be: human.

The bursting dam meant Erica Durance once again had to confront her phobia and endure being submerged in water. "It's just something I have to deal with now," Durance sighs. "You've got to go for it. If your character has to do it, you've got to do it. It's kind of like Murphy's Law," she laughs. Fortunately, the *Smallville* crew did everything they could to ensure she was comfortable. "They do a really good job here," she says. "Unless you're outside in a lake that's frozen and they can't do anything about it, they usually warm up the water for you, so it wasn't bad."

For Allison Mack, the watery sequence presented a different set of challenges, as it came towards the end of a fourteen-day fast. "I hadn't eaten solid food for eleven days," she admits, "and the last three days of my cleanse happened to be the three days that we were shooting being dragged through water and mud. So not only was I starving, but I was frail and weak. It was not pleasant!"

Opposite: This drawing was created in a later episode as Lex was searching for his rescuer.

# BIZARRO

'Sober' by Kelly Clarkson

Another strange experience Mack had to cope with during this episode was having her character wake up in a morgue. "I found that weird, but it wasn't as bad as being buried alive back in season one — that was worse," she confirms. "The morgue wasn't so bad, because it was actually quite spacious inside." Once Chloe revived, she learned from Clark that Lana had died. "That was a challenging scene," Mack recalls, "because it started out really emotional, but then it moved directly into exposition, so it was like I had to mourn Lana's death and then tell the audience the story all in one breath."

## CHLOE: This guy can fly? God, Clark, you've got to get on that one.

On a more humorous note, Lois got to see a new side of "Clark" in a sequence where Bizarro comes on to her. "Wasn't that shocking?" Erica Durance laughs. "Those little things are always fun, because you get to play and tease the audience a little bit and foreshadow their relationship in the future. It's always fun to play that comedic side of it, and it took Lois by surprise, of course, because she isn't privy to the information everyone else seems to know by this point." Durance believes, however, that Lois would never have taken such advances seriously. "Lois thinks, 'Okay, this is a friend, and sometimes he's a nuisance,'" she explains. "Sometimes she thinks he does things that are cute, but she knows he loves Lana, and I really think that's where *she* thinks he's at, that he was just dealing with that tragedy. So, Lois was just saying 'Okay, you know what? I took one for the team, okay? Do it again, and maybe I won't believe you, but this time, it's okay.' So she lets him get away with it."

The Martian Manhunter's assistance to Clark is a holdover from the sixth season finale, 'Phantom', and in this season première, John Jones continues to watch out for Kal-El as Clark's Kryptonian father would have wished. "Clark needed help to stop Bizarro," Phil Morris explains. "He doesn't know how to deal with these types of threats to him or his human charges. John has a sense of what it's all about, and where it comes from, while Clark/Kal-El has no clue. So John steps in and gives Clark the benefit of his wisdom and knowledge of this creature that has no empathy, no sympathy, and no sense of humanity. He is also there to physically help Clark by scooping Bizarro up and taking him away."

Kara's underwater rescue of Lex echoed Clark's watery rescue in the very first episode of *Smallville*. "You can never go wrong with doing a throwback to the pilot," episode writer Kelly Souders laughs. Writer Todd Slavkins adds, "There was an irony that both members of the House of El would be destined to save Lex at first, but I think Lex probably should have learned [back then] that he should stay away from large bodies of water!"

Michael Rosenbaum also enjoyed this echo from the show's beginnings. "It's typical, isn't it?" he says with a laugh. "Everything comes back around again. In the pilot episode, Lex is saved by Clark, and now, six years later, he's saved by Clark's cousin, and there's water involved as I almost drown in a car. It's very symbolic." ■

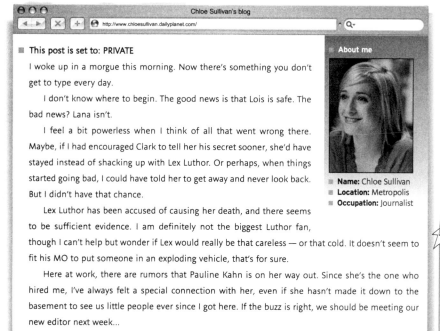

**Chloe Sullivan's blog**

http://www.chloesullivan.dailyplanet.com/

■ **This post is set to: PRIVATE**

I woke up in a morgue this morning. Now there's something you don't get to type every day.

I don't know where to begin. The good news is that Lois is safe. The bad news? Lana isn't.

I feel a bit powerless when I think of all that went wrong there. Maybe, if I had encouraged Clark to tell her his secret sooner, she'd have stayed instead of shacking up with Lex Luthor. Or perhaps, when things started going bad, I could have told her to get away and never look back. But I didn't have that chance.

Lex Luthor has been accused of causing her death, and there seems to be sufficient evidence. I am definitely not the biggest Luthor fan, though I can't help but wonder if Lex would really be that careless — or that cold. It doesn't seem to fit his MO to put someone in an exploding vehicle, that's for sure.

Here at work, there are rumors that Pauline Kahn is on her way out. Since she's the one who hired me, I've always felt a special connection with her, even if she hasn't made it down to the basement to see us little people ever since I got here. If the buzz is right, we should be meeting our new editor next week...

**About me**

■ **Name:** Chloe Sullivan
■ **Location:** Metropolis
■ **Occupation:** Journalist

**DID YOU KNOW?**

The secret of Lana's survival was successfully kept for most of the summer preceding the screening of the season première.

# KARA

**WRITTEN BY:** Todd Slavkin & Darren Swimmer
**DIRECTED BY:** James Conway

**GUEST STARS:** Michael Cassidy (Grant Gabriel), Terence Stamp (Voice of Jor-El), Richard Keats (Doctor), Kim Coates (Agent Carter), Theresa Lee (Lab Technician), Dean Redman (Policeman), Peter Bryant (Lex's Assistant), Tom McBeath (Lex's Lawyer)

**DID YOU KNOW?**

Months before taking the role of Grant Gabriel, Michael Cassidy could be seen on The CW show *Hidden Palms*.

Lois returns to Reeves Dam to survey the site with Clark in tow. There, they discover what appears to be an interstellar craft adorned with Kryptonian symbols, before something breezes through and knocks Lois out. Clark sees that their attacker is a superpowered blond female who flies away before he can learn her identity.

While trying to convince Lois that she didn't see anything in the woods, Clark tries to find out who the mysterious girl could be, unaware that *she* is looking for *him*, as well. They eventually find one another and Clark learns that she is Kara, his cousin from the planet Krypton who was awakened from suspended animation after the dam burst. She is surprised to see that he is fully grown, as she was expecting to find a baby. Kara urges Clark to help her find her ship, or there could be disastrous consequences.

Meanwhile, Lex is cleared of any charges for Lana's murder after "a disgruntled LuthorCorp employee" confesses to the crime. Lex doesn't truly believe Lana is dead, and he manages to locate her in Shanghai. He confronts her and assures her that he will not hurt her again.

Lois's insistence that she saw something in the woods gets the attention of the *Daily Planet*'s new editor, Grant Gabriel, who tells Lois that if she can deliver a story on the spaceship, she can have a job. Though her story is not printed, she still lands a job at the *Daily Planet*, and another legend begins...

## CLARK: Chloe, not only is she as strong as I am — she can fly.
## CHLOE: Whoa. Sounds like we've got ourselves a true-blue supergirl.

The appropriately titled 'Kara' formally introduced Kara Zor-El to the *Smallville* mythos and sent her character on a quest to find her cousin. "Zor-El had sent her to find baby Kal-El, because he knew that Kal-El had left Krypton and landed on Earth," episode writer Todd Slavkin explains. "She was supposed to find the baby and destroy him," his co-writer Darren Swimmer adds.

Early speculation had fans wondering if Kara had been introduced with a spin-off television series in mind. "Honestly, the spinning off of Supergirl was never an intention," Al Gough says. "If you're going to spin off a show, you spin it off after season four or five; season seven is just too late. We brought in Kara because we wanted Clark to get a glimpse of what his life had been like on Krypton from somebody who had actually grown up there. We liked the idea that she was an older cousin on Krypton who was then

*Opposite: Kara keeps Lois and Clark from getting any closer to her ship.*

## SUPERGIRL!

Clark's cousin Kara, better known to comic book enthusiasts as Supergirl, first appeared in issue #252 of *Action Comics*, published in 1959.

Initially, Superman kept the existence of his superpowered cousin a secret, and Supergirl would stop crimes in secret. Kara's original secret identity was an orphan named Linda Lee, who took the last name Danvers after being adopted. Rather than a pair of glasses concealing her true identity, Linda would hide behind a brunette wig.

The original version of Supergirl remained until DC's *Crisis on Infinite Earths*, where she died in an attempt to save the multiverse. In the years following, DC Comics made several attempts to recreate Supergirl, including a shape-shifting "Matrix" life form and the daughter of Superman and Lois from a potential future. In 2004, the Kara Zor-El version of Supergirl resurfaced and was brought back to regular comic book continuity, spearheaded by writer Jeph Loeb, who also worked on *Smallville* for three seasons.

*Smallville* hinted at Supergirl with the arrival of "Kara" in the third season finale, 'Covenant'. While this character turned out to be a human named Lindsay, it's possible that she may have been imbued with some of the Kryptonian Kara's essence.

The cover to Supergirl's first comic book appearance in 1959 asked "Is she friend or foe?" Nearly fifty years later, The CW's first promotional advertisement featuring Kara would ask the same question, and Laura Vandervoort would bring Supergirl a new life in live action.

the younger cousin when she got to Earth, as this put Clark into a sort of mentor situation with a new kind of super hero, and we could also get some comedy out of it, too."

In addition to the iconic moment of Clark meeting his superpowered cousin, this episode is notable for being Lois Lane's first foray into a career at the *Daily Planet*. "Up until that point, you saw her dipping into journalism and becoming a reporter," Erica Durance notes. "She's always had a really curious mind, and this was one of the first times she saw something and thought, 'You know what? This is going to be a big discovery.' That's what feeds her to go after her dream to discover things and be the first one to crack a story."

### CLARK: How many times do I have to tell you, Lois? You slipped in the mud, you hit your head on a rock. I was the one who helped you to your feet. Why do you think I've got mud all over me?

Durance believes that Lois got her job at the *Daily Planet* on her own merit. "The tendency is to always make a joke of it," she says. "But, you know what, her work speaks for itself. People will draw whatever conclusions they like, but you know that in the future she ends up becoming a very, very good journalist. The difference is that after she got the job, she and Grant started having a little bit of a fling, but before she got the job, there was no fling. I think he found her interesting, but he is so hard-nosed that he would never hire somebody that would make him look bad."

Durance enjoyed the vibrant dynamic between Lois and Grant Gabriel. "Everything's very much a mental challenge between them," she explains. "They have all this fun repartee, but it's all about wordplay, smarts and the job." She also thinks that Lois's relationship with the successful Grant sows the seeds of her character's legendary ambition. "Here's this young guy, who's already the editor of the *Daily Planet*, and he represents something that Lois would like to be. She's just getting over her relationship with Oliver. Her heart is broken, so she's not really interested in a relationship. He's just somebody she finds fun and interesting. She's trying to be carefree and doesn't want to be too intense."

Allison Mack thinks that her cousin's sudden arrival at the *Daily Planet* was too overwhelming for Chloe. "She wants very badly to be happy for Lois, but on the other hand, she's like, 'Wait a minute, this isn't okay,'" she says. Several of Chloe's problems stem from the appointment of the *Planet*'s new editor. "She doesn't like him," Mack confirms. "He's not nice to her; he's totally dismissive and completely condescending."

Writer Holly Harold feels Grant's dismissive attitude toward Chloe is warranted. "He's got a point," she notes. "He pushes Chloe to be a better journalist, but he sees something in Lois that intrigues him. Lois is more of a rebel, I think. Not that Chloe doesn't go after a story, but she's a little more covert. Lois is the one to bust down the door and head in all guns blazing, and I think that really appeals to Grant." ∎

Above: Clark and his newly discovered cousin, Kara Zor-El.

Below, left: A production artist's rendering of Kara's spaceship.

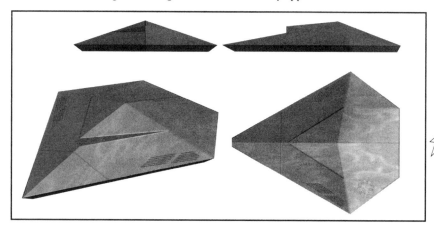

**DID YOU KNOW?**

Laura Vandervoort was born on September 22, 1984, nearly two months before the release of the original *Supergirl* film.

# FIERCE

**WRITTEN BY:** Holly Harold
**DIRECTED BY:** Whitney Ransick

**GUEST STARS:** Michael Cassidy (Grant Gabriel), Eva Marcille (Tyler Crenshaw), Elisa King (Carly), Christine Chatelain (Tempest Grace), Kim Coates (Agent Carter), Robert Thurston (Emcee), Peter Bryant (Lex's Henchman)

Seeking a way to fit into normal life on Earth, Kara enters the Miss Sweet Corn Beauty Pageant during Smallville's annual Harvest Festival. There she encounters three meteor-infected pageant contestants, Tempest, Tyler, and Carly, who are really in town seeking hidden treasure. They use their weather-related powers to make sure they get what they want. Kara attempts to foil them and winds up in jail. They use her map to track down the treasure, and when Clark tries to stop them they unearth a kryptonite medallion, weakening him. Kara breaks out of jail and turns up just in time to save her cousin. She destroys the kryptonite with her heat vision.

Back at the farm, Clark juggles with the responsibility of protecting his newly-arrived cousin and the complicated feelings associated with his reunion with Lana, who returns to town alive and apparently well. Meanwhile, Lex becomes fixated on discovering the identity of the angelic blond woman who rescued him from his flooded vehicle...

## KARA: Maybe fitting in won't be so bad after all.

"Kara wanted to fit in," episode writer Holly Harold notes, explaining why they decided to have Kara enter a beauty contest. "She wanted to be a part of this new world, and what better way to seize it? Kara is different from Clark. She wouldn't be like Clark, hiding under a bushel of corn, so to speak, and there are lines in the episode suggesting Clark doesn't live the most scintillating life. She's a girl who puts herself out there, and in a way she's trying to capture that teenage wish fulfillment that has always been an embodiment of the ostracized teenager of Smallville. Bringing that out again with Kara was a perfect play on that."

Kara's competition — Tempest, Tyler, and Carly — had the ability to control heat, cold, and wind, and their combined powers could put a stop to anyone who dared cross them. For the sequence where Jimmy is frozen inside his car, special effects supervisor Mike Walls reveals that most of it was done using physical effects. "For the white look, we used wax blown onto the car through high-pressure guns," he recalls. "For the windows frosting up, we used Crystal Frost, which you use to frost-up your windows at Christmastime. Then, we hit it with heat guns, to accelerate it a bit." Physical effects were also used to "freeze" some of the less fortunate beauty queens. "The makeup department did a really fantastic job on their skin, and then we froze them up around the edges with the wax," Walls reveals.

A sequence where Clark teaches Kara how to hone her powers is a throwback to the early days of the series when Clark would practice his powers on the farm, usually with his father, Jonathan. "It was a little bit of a shout out to the stuff that Al and Miles had set up

Opposite: Kara dresses as a magician in a deleted scene from 'Fierce'.

'Glamor Queen' by Boink
'You're A Bomb' by Boink
'Oh Baby Blue' by Homy
'Gained the World' by
Morcheeba
'Mind Full of Daggers' by
Juliette & The Licks

from the early seasons, when Clark was learning do to things, and what he went through," Harold says. "I think he's proven himself to be really good as a mentor. Tom Welling is great at playing that kind of role, so that's always fun to do."

Laura Vandervoort enjoyed playing the scenes with Kara and Clark as well. "Tom's great," she enthuses. "He's a great actor, and he's really helped me with some of the dialogue. When I'm not sure how to play it, he's always there to support me and give me ideas, and on camera he's always teaching me, like an older brother teaching a younger sister."

'Fierce' also involved some wild outfits for Kara, including a sequence where she had to wear a bikini. "I've never worn a bathing suit on camera," says Vandervoort, "so of course, like any young girl, I was kind of self-conscious and unsure if I was ready to do that. But they made sure I was comfortable, and it was used in a comedic way, so I was okay with it."

Lana was believed to be dead by most of the series' regular characters for the first two episodes of the season. During this episode Kristin Kreuk's character was brought back to town and quickly reunited with Clark. Holly Harold relished the chance to explore this meeting. "That was really fun to write, because it was an emotionally overwhelming moment for Clark: Lana wasn't dead, but he was also wondering, 'How could you have

**DELETED SCENE!**

Unfortunately as time sometimes limits what can fit into a *Smallville* episode, some moments are planned but are then missing from the final cut. From the original script of 'Fierce' by Holly Harold...

CLARK
Wait. I think I have a story Gabriel will appreciate.
            (off her interest)
It's about Lana...

CHLOE
Clark, covering my best friend's murder was the most difficult thing I've ever done. I can't —

Chloe looks up, unable to believe her eyes. Lana stands at the bottom of the stairs.

CHLOE
Oh my God...

Tears starting to stream, she rushes to hug her best friend.

CHLOE
You're alive!
(to Clark)
And you knew?!

CLARK
Only for a day. I'm sorry, Chloe.

LANA
It's my fault. I swore him to secrecy.

Chloe pulls back, wiping away her tears of joy.

CHLOE
Remind me to be furious with both of you. Later.

Above: Kara's beauty contest win is interrupted by Smallville police.

done this to me?' It was a double-edged sword. He was devastated from losing her. There was that instantaneous joy of that heart-stirring moment, but there was also a lot to recover from, and Clark was justifiably angry."

**LEX: Twice I've been pulled back from the brink of death, and both times it was by a member of the Kent family. I'm not a man who believes in coincidences. Sooner or later, I'll find out the truth. Are you a savior? Or are you a warning?**

Harold reveals that she and the other writers believed that it was important for Lana to come back to the series as early in the season as possible. "We thought it wasn't soon enough," Harold laughs. "Part of the reason anybody tunes in regularly to a television show is to see the characters they're familiar with and love, and dropping any character out for too long is always a bad idea because people get frustrated and worry they aren't going to come back."

A sequence where Chloe learned about her friend Lana's survival was cut from the episode. Harold recalls why this happened: "We wanted it to be a tender, wonderful scene, but because the episode ended up being so large with all the effects and the whole beauty pageant, we realized we weren't doing the sequence justice at all."

Despite the episode getting good ratings in key demographics 'Fierce' was one of Al Gough's least favorite entries from the seventh season. "There are times when you're trying to service other aspects of having a series on a network, such as product placements and tying into other shows, where it just doesn't work," Gough says. "The female [ratings] numbers were great on that episode, which is bizarre, because it was terrible." ∎

**DID YOU KNOW?**

Guest star Eva Marcille was the winner of the third cycle of the reality television series *America's Next Top Model*.

# CURE

**WRITTEN BY:** Al Septien & Turi Meyer
**DIRECTED BY:** Rick Rosenthal

**GUEST STARS:** Dean Cain (Dr. Curtis Knox), Phil Morris (John Jones/The Martian Manhunter), Jovanna Huguet (Sasha Woodman), Jason Poulsen (Jimmy's Co-Worker), Natalia Minuta (Sophia)

The revelation that a former classmate turned meteor freak has been cured of her affliction leads Chloe to a meeting with her doctor, Curtis Knox. However, Knox's treatment is controversial and has side effects — it causes people to forget major blocks of time. He is also secretly harvesting their meteor-enhanced body parts to prolong the life of his mortal love, Sophia.

Knox had been in the employ of Lex's 33.1 project until Lex discovered some of his test subjects had been found dead. Lex confronts Knox about this, then shoots him. Knox gets up and knocks out Lex — then Clark appears and rescues Lex.

Chloe goes to Dr. Knox for treatment, but when she suspects something is up Knox chloroforms her — he wants to harvest her heart so that Sophia can live forever. Clark arrives just before Knox is about to undergo the procedure on Chloe. The men fight inside Knox's laboratory, and the ensuing battle accidentally shuts off Sophia's life-support system, and she dies. Later John Jones tells Clark he has disposed of Knox.

Unknown to Clark, Lana begins setting up a headquarters in Metropolis for her Isis Foundation, which also houses a secret back room full of surveillance equipment to keep tabs on Lex...

## CLARK: You're going to forget everything! You're going to forget your friends, your experiences... you're going to forget me. You're going to forget me!

It was a thrill for the episode's writers to have the actor who played Superman for four seasons on the TV series *Lois & Clark* playing the villainous Dr. Curtis Knox. "To have the two Supermen fight each other was a real kick," Al Septien enthuses, "and Dean Cain did a great job. It was fun to use a [past] Superman in a different way. The other [Superman alumni] that we'd used previously had all turned up as good characters on our show. Here was a chance to have a former Superman show up as a bad guy, which was a really nice twist."

Turi Meyer explains their vision for the character: "Curtis Knox was immortal. He'd lived for centuries and had fallen in love many times. He had had to watch them all grow old and die, and then for this one woman he found a way." Al Septien continues: "He found a technology when he started testing meteor freaks. He concocted a collection of organs that when transplanted would give her immortality, or something close. His goal was to find the right meteor-infected organs, ending with the heart — which happened to be Chloe's — that had such a high level of meteor concentration that it would've allowed his bride to live much longer than any other woman could, so she would be the perfect match for him."

*Opposite: Dr. Knox is determined to save the life of his beloved Sophia.*

The lesson of possible immortality would resonate with Clark. "It's better for him to learn sooner rather than later that he's going to have to deal with it," Meyer says. "The idea of seeing Curtis Knox weep over the woman he loves and realizing that that's going to be him someday, I think, resonates in the episode."

Phil Morris believes that his character, John Jones, could understand the trials that Knox has gone through. "John has also formed a bond with someone who he is ultimately going to outlive," he explains. "The first few times I'm sure he was very sad — how do you go on, knowing that you're going to outlive everybody you know? But John has come to terms with it. I think he encourages Clark not take for granted the relationships and bonds that he creates, because they are so temporary. They're temporary for us, as humans, so they're ultimately even more fleeting for beings that are quasi-immortal."

Morris believes that John Jones was aware of Knox for generations. "John Jones is a manhunter; he's a detective and he's quasi-immortal like Knox, so he has probably been chasing Knox for a long time," he muses, "or at least has been aware of his various guises and realizes that he is very evil and very dangerous."

## LOIS & CLARK: THE NEW ADVENTURES OF SUPERMAN

Nearly a decade before *Smallville* hit TV screens, the 1990s shed a different light on the Superman story with the TV show *Lois & Clark: The New Adventures of Superman*.

Initially devised as a Superman story from the perspective of Lois Lane, series creator Deborah Joy LeVine focused primarily on the "love triangle between two people." On *Lois & Clark*, Lois (played by *Desperate Housewives*'s Teri Hatcher) was completely enamored with Superman — and barely noticed her frequent journalistic partner Clark Kent. Through four seasons, the *Daily Planet*'s top reporters crossed paths with villains such as Lex Luthor, the time-traveling Tempus, and Intergang. Their relationship also blossomed, with Lois eventually learning Clark's secret and the couple getting married. Former football player Dean Cain played *Lois & Clark*'s Clark Kent. An Elvis-loving Perry White was played by the late Lane Smith, and Jimmy Olsen was played by two different actors — Michael Landes for the first season, and Justin Whalin thereafter.

The series' final episode ended with a cliffhanger, and many fans wondered where the story would go next. Executive producer Brad Buckner later revealed the producers' plans to resolve the series-ending cliffhanger: "The little boy [left behind] began to grow at an abnormal rate, turning into a preteen in a matter of a few months. He also began to develop superpowers, not all of which he used responsibly, since he was a troubled kid. It turns out he was Kryptonian royalty, stashed by his mother to keep him safe from assassins. In the end he had to (tearfully) leave the only parents he'd ever known (Lois and Clark) and return to save his imperiled people."

'Cure' also provided conflict for Kara, who sped off after it appeared to her that her cousin was siding with John Jones. "Her father told her never to trust the Martian Manhunter," Laura Vandervoort explains, "so her immediate reaction is to get him out of the picture. When she finds out he is actually friends with Clark, she starts to question Clark's intentions, and she's obviously very confused. His appearance really shakes her foundations."

Above: TV's Clark Kent of the nineties meets TV's Clark Kent of today.

## KNOX: I *was* Jack the Ripper.

Dean Cain was also popular among his co-stars. "Dean was amazing to work with," says Michael Rosenbaum. "He's a really good guy, and there was no ego, he was there to have fun. He talked highly of me in an article, and I really thank him for that," Rosenbaum laughs. "We had a lot of laughs, and he has a lot of good stories. He appreciates what he has and what he's done, and I think he's very grateful. He was fun to work with."

Cain's presence in 'Cure' was also memorable for first assistant director Mairzee Almas. "What a nice guy," she says. "He has a lot of respect for the whole Superman mythology, and I think he really enjoyed getting to play a bad guy. I think it was fun for him, and a bit of an inside joke — to revisit Superman and play someone else."

A touching moment near the conclusion of the episode marked the end, for the time being, of Chloe and Jimmy's relationship. "That last scene was an amazing experience," Allison Mack recalls. "Aaron Ashmore is so talented and so present for the people he works with. Rick Rosenthal was our director, and he did an amazing job, really helping us and stopping us to breathe and all of that sort of stuff. It was a fun scene." ■

**DID YOU KNOW?**

Phil Morris (John Jones) portrayed the DC Comics villain Vandal Savage, who, like Curtis Knox, is immortal, in the *Justice League Unlimited* animated series.

# ACTION

| WRITTEN BY: Caroline Dries | GUEST STARS: Christina Milian (Rachel Davenport), Michael |
|---|---|
| Directed By: Mairzee Almas | Cassidy (Grant Gabriel), Christopher Jacot (Ben Meyers), David Richmond-Peck (Director), Michael Stevens (Talent Agent), Morgan Brayton (Marilyn), Anna Galvin (Gina) |

A film crew has chosen Smallville as the location for a movie based on the comic book *Warrior Angel*. The set becomes dangerous when the film's star, Rachel Davenport, finds her life threatened. Fortunately, Clark is available for a quick rescue when the brakes on Rachel's car are cut.

Clark rescues Rachel again by stopping a bullet in midair. This feat is witnessed by her attacker, Ben, a production assistant from the picture who feels that the movie's happy ending damages the original continuity of the comics, where Penelope was destined to die so Warrior Angel could fulfill his destiny. Ben recognizes Clark as a super hero and decides that Lana must die in order for Clark to embrace his future. He throws her from the balcony of Oliver's penthouse, but Clark arrives in time to stop her fall.

Lois discovers that LuthorCorp has purchased land near Reeves Dam with only a cabin on it and decides to investigate. She heads to the LuthorCorp offices to uncover more information, where she is caught by Lex. Lex uses Lois's notes to find the cabin, where he discovers that Lionel is being held captive by a woman named Marilyn — who is in the pay of Lana. Marilyn pulls a gun on Lex, but Lionel knocks her out.

After the movie wraps, Rachel gives Clark a gift — a cape prop from the film. Lex visits Ben in Belle Reve to find out what he really saw, but Ben keeps Clark's secret.

## CLARK: I guess I never really got into comic books.

The discovery that the Luthors owned some land near Reeves Dam sent Lois on a story that ultimately helped Lex to find his captive father. Lois's sleuthing even put her in a disguise as she snuck into LuthorCorp to try to find answers. Director Mairzee Almas enjoyed putting that sequence together. "That was fun," she smiles, "and a great foreshadowing of what Lois will become and how she will behave and use her smarts to get through any situation." Erica Durance agrees, "They brought in a couple of little story arcs this season where I go undercover," she notes, "and what I love is, because I'm not in every episode, but whether I am or I'm not on screen, Lois is always just continuing to work on her main focus at the *Daily Planet* — namely going after Lex. They kept that going throughout the whole season, which was really fun. This is the first time she's alluded to going after him, and the first time she decides, 'I'll dress up and go undercover.' And that's what reporting is, right? I thought it was just really fun and it was so great to work with Michael Rosenbaum."

Lois's undercover jaunt was also a favorite moment of episode writer Caroline Dries. "I loved the shot of Lois walking into Lex's office totally calm and collected," she says.

*Opposite: Rachel Davenport has a gift for the man who saved her life.*

'Dirty Little Rockstar' by The Cult

# WARRIOR ANGEL!

*Smallville*'s art department created the many *Warrior Angel* comic book covers that have been seen in episodes over the years. Property master Aleya Naiman explains the process: "What we usually do is take existing comic books that are an appropriate size, then the art department will do the artwork for it. We'll get it approved, and then we'll send it to a printing house that has that same sort of glossy paper that's used for comic book covers. We'll usually create a cover and then some inside pages, because you'll want to see the front and the back, and often they'll want to show someone flipping through it. We've got to make sure that the artwork on the inside is also something that we've generated, so that we don't get into trouble for showing an actual, uncleared comic book."

"Action" Episode #6    Warrior Angel Cut-Out Concept

"We see her in this cool Prada suit, and she just walks right in and goes to his computer. You know she's nervous, but she just does it. Anytime we can get different characters to cross paths is great. We don't see Lois and Lex together that much, so anytime we can get interactions like that, it works to our advantage."

Lois' investigation into Luthor property was against the wishes of her editor at the *Daily Planet*, Grant Gabriel. "Grant was obviously trying to throw her off," Dries notes, "because he's trying to protect his secret with Lex, but Lois ends up, as usual, opening a can of worms."

Lois's use of the alias 'Susie Blodgett' had its origins in a classic 1959 issue of *Superman's Girlfriend, Lois Lane*. The nod to the comic book was intentional. "I know my Lois," Dries laughs. She confirms the episode's inspiration and reverence to the show's fandom. Dries was surprised by some of the online response. "It was funny, the fan reaction," she recalls. "Half of them were insulted, and half of them were impressed. Those are exactly who our fans are, they're so serious about the show that it's hard to step away and be like, 'Oh, that's me.' But we love them for it — it's this funny relationship we have with our fans."

Above: Clark and Lana read the note attached to Rachel's gift.

## LOIS (to Grant): Oh, for the record, if I'd been your plus one, you would have been my arm candy.

In showing the production of a Warrior Angel film, 'Action' offered a chance to take a peek into what *Smallville* the show is like behind the scenes, though a conscious effort was made to ensure the references were not too "insider". "There was a danger of putting in too many in-jokes for those of us that work on films, that the real world would not get or understand," explains Almas, "so my challenge was to keep the excitement level around the movie high, and not fall into any in-jokes. I tried to stay true to the rules of a film set, but I didn't get into the real technical aspects, like, for example, how a prop guy would really behave around a gun. We took license with that, and we did it for dramatic reasons, but I think it works."

In addition to keeping the story as accessible as possible, the show's production team strove to make sure the Warrior Angel movie sets constructed for the episode didn't ruin the illusion of the series. Production designer James Philpott explains: "There was a bit of concern with making things look like movie sets because we were obviously filming on our own sets and locations. We were really conscious about making sure if it was actually a 'set' set for the show that the audience would never see behind it, so that we always played out of built sets as locations, rather than as sets for the movie, so that they still could function as real places in Smallville on-screen."

# ACTION

**DID YOU KNOW?**

*Warrior Angel* comics were first mentioned on-screen in *Smallville* during the season one episode 'Stray'.

As well as bringing the Warrior Angel legend to life, 'Action' is noteworthy for its rescue scenes right from the start, when Clark first saved Rachel's life as her car flies through the air. "That was actually pretty intricate stuff," special effects supervisor Mike Walls recalls. "There was a lot of debate about how we were going to show Clark making the save, because we had the car flying through air and that was all done practically, as a gag. We basically separated all of the elements into three different, specific action sequences. We had a stunt man driving the car at fifty mph, and he went up the pipe ramp, flipped the car and landed it. As he went through the air, the car corkscrewed off the pipe ramp, and then as it hit a certain mark, we blew the doors off on both sides — which would be Clark going in and out. When it landed and that part was over, we dragged the car and blew it up as we were dragging it, so you'd get the car exploding. Finally, they did the close-up shots against green screen of Tom grabbing the girl and coming into position, then they just melded it back. They put a camera right where we figured the car was going to land so it would look like he was right in front of the car as it came over the top of his head."

Another rescue came away from a movie set as Clark rescued Lana as she fell from Oliver's penthouse. "That was very simple stuff," Walls remembers. "In the end, we hung Kristin on wires and just let her fall back into a natural position, with the camera looking at her, and then we did Tom coming straight down toward the camera lens. We also did a shot where Tom holds out his arms, and we just dropped her into them." The show's

## Smallville 🐓 Ledger

✷ ✷ ✷ ✷ ✷ ✷ ✷ ✷ ✷ ✷ ✷ ✷ ✷ ✷

### ACTION!

Hollywood comes to Smallville on Saturday as production will begin on WA Pictures' multi-million dollar *Warrior Angel* film.

The movie, which stars Tim Wellington (*Abby the Judge*, *The Mist*) and Rachel Davenport (*Sunset Hills*, *I Said I Loved You*) has chosen the one-theater town of Smallville as the backdrop for their super hero action. *Warrior Angel* is based on the Fantasy Comics hero introduced in 1938, and promises a "new take" on the classic mythos. Acclaimed director Monty Smith (*Convenience Store*) is helming the picture.

The production is expected to bring some much-needed cash reserves to Smallville, which is still repairing its infrastructure after the second meteor shower which rocked the town in 2005. Businesses should also expect a pick-up in commerce as the film's 200+ crew members will be taking up residence over the next six weeks.

Keep reading *The Ledger* for exclusive reports as this exciting production sweeps through town.

By George "The Streak" Talmer

crew had already crushed the vehicle that cushioned their landing. "They just stood on top of a car that we'd pre-crashed. We dropped a block on a car and said, 'That'll be Tom, right there,'" he reveals with a laugh.

The gory scene where Lionel pulls his hand out of a steel trap was created by casting a duplicate of John Glover's real hand. "There was my skin, and then there was the blood," Glover explains, "and they put the replica of my skin over it, so there was this kind of bloody thing underneath, so as I pulled it out, you could see it cut through the fake flesh, and the blood would start to ooze."

### LANA: Millions of people look up to Warrior Angel. What if those people could look up to you instead?

The filming of a *Warrior Angel* movie was something *Smallville*'s writers had wanted to do for years. It almost happened late in the sixth season, but a similar episode on the show's Thursday night companion series on The CW had prevented it from happening.

Above: Someday Clark may realize exactly what he can do with a red cape...

"*Supernatural* was doing a movie episode at the same time, and we didn't want to have two of those on the same night," Caroline Dries reveals.

*Smallville*'s casting directors went to singer and actress Christina Milian to play Rachel Davenport, the *Warrior Angel* movie's lead actress. "She was lovely," Mairzee Almas recalls. "What a wonderful kid she was! Just great. She was a nice spark of energy. You know, I think we at *Smallville* can be a little intimidating at first, as a family of people, and a crew and a cast that have been working together for so long, that I think it's so difficult for any guest star when they're first coming in, but everybody works so hard to make our guest stars feel welcome and at home."

'Action' concluded with the iconic imagery of Clark holding Warrior Angel's red cape — a harbinger of his own future. "That's a pretty clear metaphor in my mind," Almas states, "particularly with how that looks with him putting it on the fence and being undecided and unsure of what he wants to do, it was just the obvious on-the-fence imagery. We really wanted the audience to see it was a cape. Christina's character gave it to Clark, and he put it on the fence, because he didn't know what to do with it yet. Everything that he ever wanted was there, on that farm, yet the inescapable pull of his destiny, which was represented by the cape... he wasn't going to escape it. But for now, he was going to put it on the fence." ■

# LARA

| WRITTEN BY: Don Whitehead & Holly Henderson DIRECTED BY: James Conway | GUEST STARS: Helen Slater (Lara), Christopher Heyerdahl (Zor-El), Heather Doerksen (Isis Receptionist), Chris Kelly (Technician), Kim Coates (Agent Carter) |
|---|---|

Kara flies to Washington, DC, in search of her missing Kryptonian crystal, which is being held and studied inside a government facility. While searching for more information, she is captured by Agent Carter from the Department of Domestic Security, who exposes Kara to Summerholt technology in hopes of learning all about her home planet. The machine awakens long-lost memories of Kara's first visit to Earth, where she recalls the warmth of her aunt Lara and learns that her father was not the noble hero she remembers him to be.

Clark finds Kara and gets his own glimpse of his family visiting the Kent home. Kara nearly dies, but Clark is able to resuscitate her with a powerful punch to the chest. As Agent Carter approaches Clark with kryptonite in hand, Lionel shoots him dead.

Clark and Kara return home and find a photo that Kara had left within a picture frame at the Kent home. Kara apologizes to Clark for the things that she has said to him, and tells him that Lara loved him very much.

Chloe visits the Isis Foundation clinic and is surprised to see that it is an organization run by Lana with her settlement money from Lex. Lana implores Chloe not to tell Clark, and Lana is assured that the conversation is off the record, though Chloe suspects that there is more to Isis than what she is being told...

## KARA: Until now, I thought he was such a god. A real Kryptonian hero. But you're right. He was nothing like that.

To gain access to the government facility, Kara relied on her sexy appearance to get her what she wanted. "Kara's beauty is one of her many strengths," episode writer Don Whitehead observes. "She's not powerful because she's beautiful, but she's willing to use her beauty to express her power. In other words, in that scene with the lab tech, she's not just some pretty girl in a red dress, she's Kara on a mission. She studied the situation, and decided this course of action is the most effective way to get the tech to tell her where the crystal is. Her initial instincts are not to hurt him or even threaten him, but to coax him into telling her what she wants to know. However, we can see in her eyes that there's a line she won't cross — she'll only take this so far. She succeeds in getting the info and his key card, but when she doesn't find the crystal, she goes back to the bar and tries a new tactic: threatening him.

"That's when Clark arrives to stop her," Whitehead continues. "We love it when she rolls her eyes at the sound of Clark's voice, because it reminds us that whether she's acting seductive or intimidating, she's still Clark's cousin Kara, just trying to do what she

Opposite: Former *Supergirl* star Helen Slater plays Clark's Kryptonian mother, Lara.

**SMALLVILLE MUSIC**

'Super Sexy Free' by
Bosshouse
'Lucid' by Eek

## SUPERGIRL: THE MOVIE

Spinning off from the popular *Superman* movie franchise starring Christopher Reeve, 1984's *Supergirl* film featured Helen Slater in the role of Kara. In this version of the story, Kara and many fellow Kryptonians survived as their home of Argo City was in a pocket of trans-dimensional space.

The film, helmed by future *Smallville* director Jeannot Szwarc, brought Kara to Earth in search of a lost device known as an Omegahedron. Once Kara gets to the planet, she creates a secret identity for herself, calling herself Linda Lee, and meets Lois Lane's sister Lucy, as well as Jimmy Olsen!

Sadly, Kara's cousin Superman is only seen on a poster in the movie, as Christopher Reeve did not appear; though Marc McClure did reprise his role of Jimmy Olsen from the *Superman* movies.

Since appearing in *Supergirl*, Slater went on to appear in the film *The Legend of Billie Jean* and guest starred on an episode of TV's *Seinfeld*. Like Christopher Reeve, Terence Stamp, Margot Kidder, and Annette O'Toole before her, *Smallville* marked Slater's return to the live-action Superman franchise.

can to retrieve the crystal, which for her at that moment feels like the only tie she has left to her father and her home."

Laura Vandervoort agrees that there's more to Kara than her sexy outfits and ability to seduce. "It's a tool that she used in that episode," she notes. "I don't think it's necessarily something she uses all of the time, but she played it up and it was what it was for that episode. But that's not who she is, and I'm sure it's bound to happen, because that's the way she is in the comic book. She's very sexy and dresses kind of scandalous when she wants certain things. But that's not who she is deep down."

### CLARK: We're not defined by our parents, Kara. One of the most important things that my adoptive parents taught me is that we shape our own destiny.

The writers of 'Lara', Don Whitehead and Holly Henderson, were thrilled to have Helen Slater feature in their episode. "In the script, we described Lara as 'luminous', and here comes Helen Slater, who is just that," says Whitehead with a smile. "We thought it was perfect casting. As they shot her, she had this sort of unearthly, radiant beauty to her."

The episode featured scenes between Lara and her niece Kara, giving screen time to two Supergirls, from both the big screen and the small screen. "I was honored to work with Helen Slater," Laura Vandervoort smiles. "I was nervous at first, because she was the original Supergirl, but she was great, and very welcoming. We talked about what it

Above: Kara uses her considerable charm to obtain information.

was like when she shot *Supergirl*, and how it's different now. We didn't really talk about the legacy; she just told me about how her life changed after she did the movie, and what I should expect."

Christopher Heyerdahl, who played Zor-El in this episode, also enjoyed spending time with the former Supergirl. He reveals that they joined forces to give their characters strong foundations. "Working with Helen Slater is always a joy," he says. "We've worked together before, and it's always great. It was fun because we really tried to figure out Lara and Zor-El's history, and we decided that they were together once upon a time, before she was with Jor-El, and that there was a very passionate, very strong relationship there, but that there was also a very passionate break-up. It didn't finish very well, and she went to Jor-El feeling that he was a man that was perhaps more well rounded in his moral beliefs. But, that passion always remained, and that was something that we tried to bring into the scene where we see them at the Kents' farm. That passion is still there, but she realizes that she cannot be with this man. She is with his brother, pregnant with their son, and it's simply not going to happen."

To create a voice for Zor-El, Heyerdahl confirms that he went for a similar sound to that he had heard from Terence Stamp as Jor-El. "They were brothers, they went to the same schools, they were educated in the same circles, in the same environment, so I wanted to bring a flavor of the El family. So trying to imitate Terence? Not at all. To bring a flavor of what he had already brought to the voice of Jor-El? Yes." ▪

**DID YOU KNOW?**

Clark's memories were explored with a similar machine at Summerholt in the season three episode 'Memoria'.

# WRATH

WRITTEN BY: Brian Peterson
& Kelly Souders
DIRECTED BY: Charles Beeson

GUEST STARS: Michael Cassidy (Grant Gabriel), Elyse Levesque (Casey Brock), Alex Zahara (Dr. Janson)

A romantic afternoon for Lana and Clark is interrupted by a mixture of kryptonite and lightning, which transfers Clark's powers to Lana. The superpowered Lana then decides to expose Lex and his atrocities. Using her new powers, Lana steals Lex's data on *Project: Scion* and offers the stolen hard drive to Grant Gabriel, hoping the *Daily Planet* will print an exposé. When Grant refuses to print an article based on stolen material, Lana attacks him and Lois. Enraged, she then confronts Lex herself and demands to be taken to the lab where *Project: Scion* is being conducted — she learns that Lex is still studying aliens.

At the lab, Lana nearly kills Lex by electrocuting him and then nearly strangles him to death before throwing him aside. Clark locates Lana and begs her to stop. They fight until a container is released and they are both weakened by kryptonite, which Clark eventually uses to reverse the process that gave Lana his powers; however, during the chaos Clark breaks a vial, accidentally releasing the liquefied form that reconstitutes Brainiac.

Lana's rage and the revelation that she has been spying on Lex forces her and Clark to discuss the strained nature of their relationship. Meanwhile, in Metropolis, a new romance is budding as Grant and Lois begin exhibiting their affection for one another...

### CLARK: Taking peoples' lives is not our choice to make.
### LANA: And how many people would still be alive if you had had the guts to get rid of Lex a long time ago?

The depth of Lana's hatred for Lex is unleashed with shocking power during this episode when she is infused with Clark's powers. "Lana truly did love Lex in many ways and really wanted the best for him," Kreuk revealed in an online interview. "She put herself on the line with her friends, saying that this is a person that she really thinks has changed, and she wanted to be part of that. When she discovered how destructive and violent he actually was, and how he was treating her, she got really angry. Her intent really was to kill him. She had planned on killing him and failed to do so, and I think she does feel in some way that to kill him would be better for the world. Yet, on the other hand, she still loves him to some degree as well. But she's coming back to Clark, the boy whom she adores, and is still good and pure and lovely, and she's not like that anymore. She's trying to be [good like Clark], because there's a part of her that's still like that. She's juggling these two sides of her character and struggling to kind of bring those two things together. It's difficult for her this season, I think, because she wants to be honest, but she also thinks there's a greater good."

Opposite: The wrath of a superpowered Lana comes with a bold new look.

Above: Lana demands that the *Daily Planet* prints an exposé on Lex Luthor.

Michael Rosenbaum laughs when he looks back on this episode. "Every year, Lana must become crazy, psychotic Super-Lana. That's just the way it is in Smallville," he sighs. "In retrospect, how cool would it have been if Lex had had those powers? Well, I guess he did, in a sense, with Zod... but that wasn't really Lex, it was Zod. Somehow, I think Kristin pulls it off. It's not an easy role to play."

**LANA: Clark, if I wanted normal, I would have rethought the part about dating a guy who shoots fire from his eyes.**

Near the episode's conclusion, Chloe has a heated conversation with Lana about the secret side of the Isis Foundation. Alison Mack notes, "When Kristin and I were rehearsing the scene, it was really important to us that it didn't come off as being catty, but very much Chloe saying, 'Listen, this is the most important person to me, and recognize that I would do anything for him. I just want you to know that that's the way I look at the situation.' I think that Lana heard that." Off-screen, Mack and Kreuk are very good friends. "I love working with Kristin," says Mack. "We have such a good time together."

SMALLVILLE MUSIC

'My Eyes' by Travis
'Spell' by Mary Digby

Episode writer Kelly Souders thinks this was an important episode for Lana to work out her feelings for her ex-husband. "['Wrath'] was certainly the culmination of the Dark Lana arc," she says. "From the pilot, Lana hasn't had an easy life. She lost her parents; she was with an aunt who left her. She's definitely had some dark things to overcome, which have always been lurking inside of her, and Lex just brought them to the surface."

Episode co-writer Brian Peterson counters: "I don't think it's necessarily that dark when you've had horrible things happen to you, to kind of take back your power and want to get vengeance." He adds that Lana still does have remaining feelings for Lex. "I don't think you could hate someone without still having feelings for them," he says.

*Project: Scion* and the liquid substance inside the vial gave the producers a chance to hint at Brainiac's return. "We knew that Brainiac was coming back," says Souders, "and instead of him just making an appearance out of the blue, we wanted to tease the audience." ∎

# HAVING THE POWER

Throughout the course of the series, almost all of Clark's friends have had superpowered experiences. Here's a look at some of them:

## LANA LANG

'Wrath' was a spotlight for what would happen if Lana had Clark's powers, but it's not her first time having a strange ability. In season one's 'Obscura', she could see through someone else's eyes; and in season four, Lana exhibited magical powers while being possessed by the witch Isobel Thoreaux.

## CHLOE SULLIVAN

In season three's 'Truth', Chloe had the temporary power of rendering everyone unable to tell a lie. Three years later, in season six, it was revealed that Chloe had a permanent meteor ability — the power to heal.

## LEX LUTHOR

Lex exhibited all of the powers of a Kryptonian for two episodes while he was the living vessel of Zod.

## PETE ROSS

When Pete made his first *Smallville* appearance in four years in the season seven episode 'Hero', meteor-enhanced chewing gum gave him a super-stretching power.

## ERIC SUMMERS

While not necessarily Clark's friend, this classmate from season one's 'Leech' took all of Clark's powers on more than one occasion.

# BLUE

WRITTEN BY: Todd Slavkin
& Darren Swimmer
DIRECTED BY: Glen Winter

GUEST STARS: Helen Slater (Lara), Christopher Heyerdahl (Zor-El), Terence Stamp (Voice of Jor-El), Mike Ennis (Paramedic), Patricia Cullen (Meteorologist)

## DID YOU KNOW?

In this episode, Grant makes a reference to a story Lois had printed in the season six episode 'Combat'.

Clark hears the call of his mother, which takes him to the Fortress of Solitude, where he places Kara's crystal into a panel and seemingly brings Lara back to life. In truth, Lara is revived through the science of Zor-El's crystal — and Zor-El has also returned, with nefarious plans.

Clark is tricked into putting on a blue Kryptonian ring — an heirloom from the House of El. Without warning, Clark finds that his powers have been drained, preventing him from stopping Zor-El, who wants to repopulate Earth with a new race of Kryptonians.

At the Fortress, Kara and Lara fight Zor-El without success, only when Clark arrives and smashes the crystal is Zor-El vanquished. Kara is transported to Detroit and wakes up on a rainy street with no memory of who she really is, and Jor-El tells Clark that he will be punished for not listening to his warnings.

Chloe and Lex learn about the relationship between Lois and Grant, and they separately urge the couple to put an end to their office romance.

## JOR-EL: Do not allow human emotions to cloud your judgment.

Christopher Heyerdahl believes that his character Zor-El's main priority was to reunite his family the way *he* wanted them to be. "I think Zor-El's ultimate agenda was to have Lara be with him," he explains, "because if they are returning to Krypton after it has been destroyed, then there is no Jor-El to compete with. He was expecting her to allow the passion and sweetness of what they had once upon a time to be much more solid in her essence after reviving her through the use of the blue crystal. He believed that this new Lara wouldn't retain the same affinity to Jor-El, and that she would be more than willing to create a new Kryptonian race on Earth and bring back their people. That, I believe, is his number one focus: to have the family he always wanted, and the hiccup, of course, is Clark not going along with it."

The mother and son reunion was very emotional for Clark and Lara. "It's very poignant to find your mother, and to see your son grown up," Helen Slater says. "I can only imagine what that would feel like. I think the effect for someone to finally know their biological mom, and to have it turn out that she's someone who is kind and warm-hearted, is probably a big, big blessing. It's the same for Lara, when she sees how Kal-El turned out, as bittersweet as it is, it's still great to know that he's thriving and a good person."

When Lara learns the truth of her survival, she is left deeply unsettled. "I'm not pleased when I find out," Slater notes. "It feels awful. At first, I'm just so happy to see my son, but when I realize the means by which I've come back, it really freaks

Opposite: Kara's father, the powerful and deadly Zor-El.

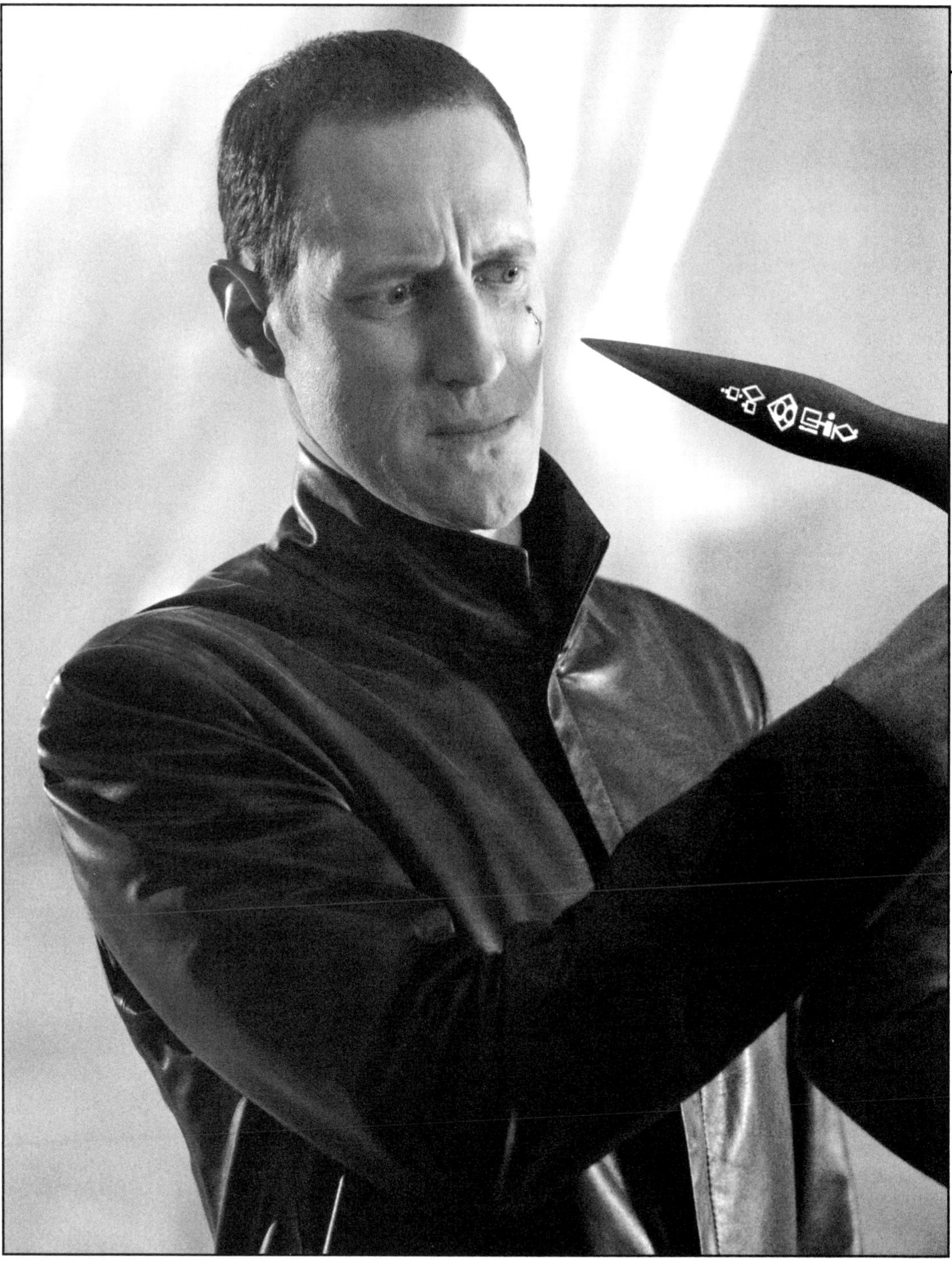

# BLUE KRYPTONITE EXPOSED!

Blue kryptonite had different effects in many comic books and media prior to appearing on *Smallville*.

In classic DC comic books, and in several video games, blue kryptonite could actually strengthen Superman and other Kryptonians; however, when blue kryptonite was used on Bizarro, it would weaken him, just as green kryptonite had a positive effect on him. In cartoons such as the 1970s Hanna-Barbera *Super Friends*, blue k was used to heal Superman from the effects of red kryptonite.

Blue kryptonite hasn't surfaced much in modern post-Crisis DC comic books; though, issue #25 of *Superman/Batman* (published in 2006) gives the colored rock a new effect: it raises Bizarro's intelligence level!

Thus far, blue kryptonite has appeared in two episodes of *Smallville* — 'Blue' and 'Persona'. It is unknown if the cobalt-hued rock will make a return appearance anytime soon...

me out. Ultimately I feel that no good that can come of it, because I know how I've been brought back."

'Blue' culminates in a dramatic confrontation in the Fortress of Solitude involving all four members of the El family. "From a narrative point of view, that's the crux of the whole storyline, where everybody is confronting everyone else," Heyerdahl explains. "There's Lara, who's allowing Kara to step in to her place, to confront her father, and the wonderful final snapping point for Zor-El and Kara, where he's actually able to take his daughter by the throat and, in his mind, teach her a final lesson of respect. Then there's Clark's decision, having to deal with destroying the crystal, knowing he's going to have to destroy the essence of his mother in order to get rid of his uncle. It's an incredible moment for Clark. The stakes are so high in that scene for everybody."

## LARA: If I emerged from this crystal, I am certain his replicant is right behind me. And he is dangerous.

The end of 'Blue' revealed that Grant Gabriel was in actuality Julian Luthor — and in the next episode, we would learn that Julian is in fact a clone of Lex's long-dead sibling. Michael Rosenbaum enjoyed that dramatic reveal. "I thought it was a cool discovery," he says. "It was out of nowhere, and I thought to myself, 'Aha! That's what I've been doing!' All of those years in the same room of the Luthor mansion, that's exactly what I've been doing, I've been looking at cloning a brother."

Above: Clark knows what he has to do...

Many fans wondered why there was no mention of Lex's other brother, Lucas, in the storyline. "Lucas is out there, but he's under Lex's control. Let's just say that," Rosenbaum laughs.

It's worth noting that even though he is well versed in dealing with Zor-El, the Martian Manhunter was nowhere to be seen. Todd Slavkin explains his absence: "There are issues in the galaxy that go beyond Clark Kent. He's an intergalactic warrior, and Clark's only one of John Jones' issues." ▪

# GEMINI

**WRITTEN BY:** Caroline Dries
**DIRECTED BY:** Whitney Ransick

**GUEST STARS:** Michael Cassidy (Grant Gabriel), Elyse Levesque (Casey Brock), Tim Guinee (Adrian Cross)

L ois receives a call from a man named Adrian who demands she tell his story or he will detonate a bomb that's attached to Chloe. Unaware of the bomb, Chloe becomes trapped in a *Daily Planet* elevator with Jimmy. Clark returns from his imprisonment in the Fortress of Solitude with a new attitude toward Lana and getting revenge against Lex. A delighted Lana opens up to Clark with all of her research.

Lois learns that Adrian is the failed product of the LuthorCorp *Project: Gemini*. She offers to print his story if he lets Chloe go, but he wants a confession from Lex. Lois heads to Grant's office where prompted by Adrian she confronts Lex about *Project:Gemini* and cloning. At Adrian's urging, she pulls a gun on Grant. Lex knocks Lois out, but her words have prompted Grant to realize that he and Adrian share the same memories, as they were both clones from the same project! Lex shoots Adrian, but this activates the bomb detonation sequence.

The one-minute countdown makes Chloe open up to Jimmy about her meteor affliction, and they kiss. Clark arrives at superspeed, just in time to dispose of the bomb.

Later, at the farm, Clark and Lana embrace, but it's not really Clark — it's Bizarro, posing as Clark. Meanwhile, the real Clark remains frozen in the Fortress of Solitude...

## ADRIAN: Just write the story. In a couple of hours, every newspaper in the country will be begging for it.

*Smallville* frequently puts its characters into unusual situations, and Michael Cassidy found being confronted by an older version of Grant Gabriel a challenge to play. "That was a really fun episode to work on," he recalls. "Tim Guinee, who played the other clone, is a great guy. I remember we went to get sushi and talked about what it might be like to see an older version of you. Do you recognize him, regardless of what he looks like? It's different to seeing an identical twin, even. You're seeing yourself. It's hard to figure out how to play a scene where the guy who's threatening your girlfriend turns out to be you!"

Creator Al Gough also enjoyed the twists and turns of this episode. "The fun of 'Gemini' was that you think it's Clark throughout the show and then you realize it's not," he says. "There are obviously hints that it's not Clark, and I think a good fan could figure out a couple of the acting choices in there. It's fun where you realize that the only reason he saved Chloe, of course, is that he needed her for information and help later."

"I was impressed that [the Bizarro reveal] didn't leak and by the fans who realized something was off," episode writer Caroline Dries marvels. "I think Tom nailed it. He played it very well; somebody pretending to be somebody else. I was so happy about that."

Dries explains that the episode was carefully planned to expose a key element of Clark and Lana's relationship. "What we wanted to do with 'Gemini' was have Lana show Clark something that she was really nervous about showing him, and was really making herself

*Opposite: Grant tries to talk Adrian down before he does anything drastic.*

'Canceling Christmas' by Michelle Featherstone
'Deck the Halls' by True Music
'Jingle Bells (Instrumental)' by Henry Stuck
'Joy to the World' by Stan Reynolds

vulnerable to Clark and his judgment," she notes. "When Clark is proud of her for taking this on by herself, Lana's really turned on by that and thinks their relationship has evolved."

As for the real Clark, freezing him away was Jor-El's way of eliminating his ties to humanity. "His idea was that Clark's love for humanity and this girl, Lana, and doing anything to protect Chloe, was distracting him," Dries says. "So if Clark was frozen until they age and die, he wouldn't be distracted when he's melted and popped back on Earth."

The central drama of the episode was Lois's struggle to save her cousin from being blown to smithereens. "When I read that script, I was really excited," Erica Durance recalls. "It was fun to work with Tim Guinee and to have that element of threat for Lois. If someone had been threatening *her*, she would have dealt with it, but the minute you bring in someone that you love, all of a sudden you're vulnerable and will do anything to save that person. Tensions were rising and rising. I thought that it was really well-written and fun episode."

# CLONING IN SMALLVILLE!
## The Luthors' Cloning Experiments

Cloning Julian was not the first example of cloning by the Luthors in the *Smallville* mythos. Here's a look at some of the past experiments gone bad...

### EMILY DINSMORE

A childhood friend of Lana's named Emily was cloned by her father and began haunting Lana in the season two episode 'Accelerate'. A side effect of the cloning experiment was that Emily could move at superspeed; she also lacked a moral center that allowed her to think capably. The clone returned a year later in season three's 'Forsaken', grown to adolescence but still unstable. It is assumed that Lionel studied Emily at Level Three during the year that she was in custody, and some of that technology may have been used in later projects.

### PROJECT: ARES

Project: Ares was intended to create the ultimate super-soldier. One of the prototypes for Project: Ares was Wes Keenan, who was imbued with the abilities of several of the meteor infected individuals in Lex's Level 33.1, as revealed in the season six episode 'Prototype'. Model 503 of Project: Ares was a clone of Lana Lang which was a discarded failure. Lana found this clone and used it to fake her own death in the sixth season finale 'Phantom'.

### PROJECT: GEMINI

Project: Gemini was the experiment that ultimately created Grant Gabriel. Lex's first, failed try at cloning his brother Julian resulted in Adrian Cross, who shared the same memories as Grant but aged at an extremely rapid rate. It is unknown how many prototypes were created before Lex successfully created Grant as a clone of Julian.

Chloe and Jimmy's incarceration in the elevator forced the characters to interact — and in the climax, Chloe finally revealed the truth about her meteor power. "I thought they were both awesome," Caroline Dries raves. "That was my favorite part of the episode. Anytime you have two characters stuck in an elevator, something's going to come out. For us, we wanted to change the dynamic between Chloe and Jimmy, and ask how this regular guy is going to deal with the fact that the girl he loves is a meteor freak. I think it worked, and it was really fun writing the dialogue for them."

Above: Backed into a corner by Adrian, Lois points a gun at Grant.

### CHLOE: I always imagined this playing out to a sad Kelly Clarkson song, not some 'Jingle Bells' muzak.

"For Jimmy and Chloe at that point in their relationship, it was a really pivotal moment," Aaron Ashmore says. "For Jimmy it kind of freed him up, to know she had told him her big secret. He does what he most wants to do — kiss her. He loves her. The truth came out because of the bomb, but it's still important *because* it was the truth."

Allison Mack enjoyed performing the elevator scene as well. "It was so much fun. It was two full days of getting to work with Aaron. It was really great," she says.

The decision to have Lex buy the *Daily Planet* was a way for the writers to bring him back into the *Smallville* fold. "As Lex is starting to burn bridges in every part of his world, we were writing a lot of scenes where it's Lex and a guest character," Caroline Dries explains. "So, storywise, we found a way to infuse Lex back into the original cast's lives, by putting him right in the middle of the activity at the *Daily Planet*. It was also a very Luthor thing to do, and a good way to create stories." ▪

### DID YOU KNOW?

Lex Luthor bought the *Daily Planet* on the TV series *Lois & Clark* as well as during certain periods of Superman comic book continuity.

# PERSONA

**WRITTEN BY:** Holly Henderson
& Don Whitehead
**DIRECTED BY:** Todd Slavkin

**GUEST STARS:** James Marsters (Brainiac), Marc McClure (Dax-Ur), Terence Stamp (Voice of Jor-El), Michael Cassidy (Grant Gabriel), Sharlene Martin (Grace), Connor Levins (Max), Tyler Hazelwood (Mugger)

## DID YOU KNOW?

Marc McClure played Marty McFly's older brother in the *Back to the Future* movie series.

Lana and Clark are enjoying a state of relationship bliss, with Lana still unaware that Bizarro has replaced the real Clark. At the Isis Foundation Lana learns from police reports that homeless people are being found dead, drained of their trace metals. She tells Bizarro Clark that she thinks these killings are connected to Brainiac. Bizarro tracks down Brainiac, hoping he can help him find a way to become Clark permanently, without the revealing effects of sunlight. Brainiac tells him that a Kryptonian living on Earth named Dax-Ur can help them.

Jor-El releases the real Clark so he can stop Bizarro. When Clark returns home, he is stunned to learn that Bizarro had taken over his life and that Lana hadn't noticed the difference.

As a ruse to obtain Dax-Ur's location, Brainiac impersonates Lionel and informs Clark that he can stop Bizarro with blue kryptonite, which he can get from Dax-Ur. Using the blue kryptonite, Clark and Lana confront Bizarro, who declares his love for Lana before being destroyed. Back at Dax-Ur's garage, Brainiac attacks Dax-Ur, siphoning his knowledge and restoring his own power, killing the Kryptonian in the process.

Grant Gabriel reveals to Lionel that he is his presumed-dead son, Julian. Father and son reunite and go out for dinner. Grant is then gunned down by a mugger — a hit ordered by Lex.

Back at the Kent farm, Clark and Lana are silently struggling to cope with what has happened.

## DAX-UR: Sometimes a scientist can get caught up in theories. My work led to the creation of the Brain Inter-Active Construct. I realized much too late that my technology could lead to the destruction of worlds.

It was Chloe, not Lana, who was the first character to notice Clark's bizarre behavior. "Chloe's the coolest," episode writer Holly Henderson says, smiling. "She has a real insight into Clark Kent; unlike Lana, who has been hurt so much the last couple of seasons that she was easily manipulated. Lana was getting a lot of things from Bizarro that were missing in her relationship with Clark, so it was easier to fool her; whereas Chloe has the distance, which made it easier for her to recognize the difference."

"Bizarro, in a way, was giving Lana the Clark she always wanted," Henderson's co-writer Don Whitehead explains. "In an earlier episode, Clark learned about the Isis Foundation and told Lana, 'We all make mistakes.' Now, Bizarro comes along and is the

Opposite: Bizarro meets a severely weakened Brainiac.

# PERSONA

Clark she's always wanted, and in a way, his attentiveness and support blinded her to the fact that it wasn't Clark."

The writers *did* concoct an explanation for Bizarro's survival, but it didn't make it into the final cut of the episode. "The eclipse in 'Blue' wasn't a real eclipse," Whitehead shares. "It wasn't about the moon blocking the sun out from Earth. It was something to do with moisture, because it was from the Fortress, and the idea was that the moisture somehow reached out beyond the Earth, maybe to Mars, which is where I think we were talking about Bizarro being taken. So, for a moment there, Bizarro didn't have the yellow sun shining down on him without any atmosphere to filter. Whatever caused that false eclipse blocked the sun out long enough for Bizarro to get his strength back and get himself out of there," he reveals.

Tom Welling used the opportunity of playing Bizarro to really flex his acting muscles. "We thought he was fantastic," Henderson says. "He did this great bit with Chloe at the *Daily Planet* where he's walking behind her, and he's kind of mimicking her. That wasn't in the script. I think he really enjoyed this episode and made it his own. To watch Tom confront Tom with these subtle differences was just amazing and really showed his range."

Below: The Kryptonian Dax-Ur lived on Earth as a human for many years.

## BIZARRO: You know he won't commit his life to you like I will. You know that.

Making his first appearance on *Smallville* since the fifth season was James Marsters as Professor Milton Fine, aka Brainiac. "I've gone from being a character who has a high amount of control to being viscous fluid, which of course means less control," James Marsters says of his character's return. "I have healed. I'm no longer viscous, but I'm not in control and I'm on the lam. The good news is that I have much cooler clothes, which means that they are more distressed and a little dirtier, which I like," he laughs.

# WHATEVER HAPPENED TO THE MAN OF TOMORROW?

The idea of a Kryptonian living on Earth as an ordinary human may have had its roots in a classic "imaginary story" first published by DC Comics in 1986.

The two-issue story was originally published in issue #423 of DC's *Superman*, and in issue #583 of *Action Comics*. They were the last issues before DC Comics initiated the Superman post-Crisis revamp by writer/artist John Byrne.

Alan Moore, a well-known British writer responsible for a memorable run on *Swamp Thing* and creator of the iconic *Watchmen*, *V for Vendetta*, and *The League of Extraordinary Gentleman*, wrote the tale in which Superman's last known days were recounted. This bookend to DC's Silver Age featured many classic elements from that era, such as the Legion of Super-Heroes, Supergirl, Krypto, and the Brainiac-Luthor team. In this continuity, it is gold kryptonite that permanently takes Superman's powers, and as an act of penance for breaking his oath not to kill, Superman voluntarily exposes himself to it. The world at large believes that Superman has died.

In truth, the man seen as Lois Lane's husband in this tale, Jordan Elliot, is in fact Superman himself, living a normal, suburban life in his new guise. In their new life, he and Lois live happily ever after.

Marc McClure, who played Jimmy Olsen in the *Superman* movies starring Christopher Reeve, was brought in to play Dax-Ur. "We wanted Clark to meet somebody who had decided to give up his powers for a woman," notes Don Whitehead, "and in finding a way to bring down Bizarro, Clark is led to Dax-Ur. The point was that Dax-Ur was a scientist who came to Earth, and, basically, he is like a Superman for a while, then he meets this woman and decides to be with her because he has fallen head over heels in love. Superman is not like that. Clark, the future Superman, is not ready to give it all up like that for one person. He absolutely is driven to always think of the welfare of the planet, of others around him, of not only the people he cares about but the people who make up the world around him, and he can never put one single person ahead of that. We wanted to show that choice of his. Dax-Ur asks who he needs the blue kryptonite for, and Clark can't answer, because it's not really for him to become human and be with Lana — it's to destroy Bizarro."

'Persona' marked the final curtain for Grant Gabriel. After reuniting and spending some father-son time with Lionel, Lex had his cloned brother eliminated. "Was it Lex?" asks Michael Rosenbaum with a grin. "What do you think? Of course it was. Clean slate. It wasn't working out the way that Lex had intended." ∎

## DID YOU KNOW?

Superman comic books feature an evil Kryptonian scientist with the very similar name of Jax-Ur.

# SIREN

**WRITTEN BY:** Kelly Souders & Brian Peterson
**DIRECTED BY:** Kevin Fair

**GUEST STARS:** Justin Hartley (Oliver Queen/Green Arrow), Alaina Huffman (Dinah Lance/Black Canary), Heather Doerksen (Receptionist)

**DID YOU KNOW?**

Alaina Huffman's previous genre credits include a run as a series regular on *Painkiller Jane*.

Chloe is moonlighting to find information for Oliver Queen about Lex when she is attacked by a vigilante known as the Black Canary, who steals a disk from her. When Black Canary tells her employer Lex about her encounter with Chloe and her rescue by Green Arrow on top of the Daily Planet building, Lex offers to pay more money if she can bring him the Emerald Archer, explaining that the Green Arrow and his friends are terrorists who have been attacking LuthorCorp facilities.

Surprised to discover that Oliver is back in town, Lois goes to his loft to find out why he hasn't called. Black Canary interrupts their reunion, and her scream shatters all of the glass throughout the penthouse, revealing Oliver's secret arsenal.

Black Canary researches Lex's claims and realizes that she has been duped. When she refuses to bring him the Green Arrow, Lex shoots her, leading to a three-way battle between himself, Green Arrow, and Black Canary, with Clark ultimately speeding in and protecting his friends from harm.

Meanwhile, Clark and Lana discuss what happened during the Bizarro affair, and Clark puts some of the mistakes from his own past on the table. Meanwhile, Lois, fresh from her discovery of Oliver's double-life, decides that she cannot share a hero with the rest of the world, and she and Oliver part for good.

**LOIS: So, in all those nights together, somewhere between brushing teeth and spooning in the sheets, you didn't think that it might be a good time to mention that you prowl the streets with green leather and a compound bow?**
**OLIVER: I don't usually bring the compound bow.**
**LOIS: Oh. So now he's a funny hero.**

In preparing for 'Siren', not only did Justin Hartley have to get into shape to wear the Green Arrow tights again — he also had to prepare for a long sequence where he is wearing very little, providing superb eye candy for his loyal fans. "When I read the script the first time, I was in a towel," Hartley recalls with a grin. "The whole thing where Lois and I were tied together by Black Canary, I was in a towel for all that, and then for three scenes in a row, it was all towel. I was like, 'Well, this is going to be something else,'" he laughs. Fortunately for Hartley, some of the scenes were changed so he got to wear a little more than just a towel.

Alaina Huffman was cast as the Green Arrow's captor and future girlfriend, Black Canary. "I thought she did a really good job," Hartley says. "She had previous

*Opposite: Chloe calls Oliver for instructions.*

experience in the same kind of genre, and she came on and had a lot of fun with the Black Canary role. They probably looked for that when they were casting, someone who would come in and own it and love it. She definitely had a lot of fun with it, and I think that's key."

Black Canary's power is in her sonic scream. Hartley remembers how entertaining that was to shoot. "It was really goofy for her," he laughs. "When you watch the show, you hear [the scream], and you see it in the effects and stuff. But on set it's the goofiest thing you've ever seen! It's a woman bending over, opening up her mouth, and nothing happens. Everyone's standing there, dead silent, except the lone jackass — me — in the background, laughing like a five-year old."

Hartley was impressed with the costume that was created for the Black Canary. "I thought it was cool, the way they did the mask," he says. "It was tricky, because it could've looked really goofy, but the way they did it with the paint instead of just doing a black mask, was a really good idea. The fishnet stockings were really cool," he adds with a smile, "because you've got to have the classic fishnet stockings for Black Canary."

## GREEN ARROW: I like the look, Italian?
## BLACK CANARY: Why? You thinking of trading in your tights?

A sequence involving the Canary scream at Oliver's apartment led to some tricky maneuvering for the shoot. Justin Hartley explains what happened: "First, they did a plate and blew the glass up with no one there," he explains, "and then they put everyone in. Erica and I had to come in and go to a different area on the stage. When we flew into the couch and then flipped over it, we had do that whole thing without the glass and everything, in front of a green screen. We were running, and I was supposed to hit the couch, take the couch with me, and then take her with me without hurting her, and *then* flip over the couch. They had a stunt couple there, and boom, the couch goes over, and it looks easy. When we went to do it, I remember specifically saying to Erica, 'You should hit the bottom of the couch, because if you hit the top of the couch, I'll run into you, and then you're going feel like you got hit by a guy.' Because I'm running full speed, you know? Anyway, she hit the bottom of the couch, I hit the top of the couch, and the couch goes nowhere, and it was like the wind got knocked out of me. The couch didn't go over, and we were just sitting there, like our lungs had collapsed. We finally figured out a way to get the couch over, but it was embarrassing to run into a couch at full speed, hit it, and then to have the soft, cushiony couch stop you. It didn't even budge," Hartley reflects, shaking his head with a smile.

Green Arrow had to juggle the affections of two women in this episode. After reading the script, Hartley says he then looked into the Green Arrow/Black Canary relationship in the comic books. "I did a lot more research on her character and on the relationship itself," he says, "because I knew it was coming, so I knew exactly what that was."

Above: Inside the *Daily Planet*, the Black Canary strikes.

Having done this research he was careful not to have his character appear attracted to Black Canary at the expense of his relationship with Lois. "It was very tricky for me, because I didn't want to disservice the relationship that he'd had with Lois before, because even though it goes against the classic mythology, I thought that Erica and I and the writers did a really good job of making it work between us. I didn't want to disservice that by coming in and going, 'Oh, look, a hot girl in a mask. Forget Lois, here we go!' At the same time, I wanted to service the script at hand, which had me kind of walking off hand in hand with her. It was very tricky, and could be a slippery slope if you get it wrong. I didn't want it to come off like, 'Oh, well, we're not dating anymore. Let me just go off with the next woman that walks through the door,'" he continues. "I wanted people when they watched it to know that it doesn't take away from the fact that they really did love each other and they really did have a real relationship. It wasn't just a physical attraction thing. The writers did a really good job with that."

'Siren' was also the episode when Lois finally learned about Oliver Queen's dual identity as Green Arrow. "When I read it I thought it was very cool, how she discovered it and then got upset with him about it," notes Hartley. "I was really happy with the way that it was written, and then I was really proud of Erica for the way she put her own twist on the writing. It was great."

Lois's discovery completely changed the way she viewed their time together. "Even once Lois understands why Oliver didn't tell her, he's still lied to her," Hartley points out. "He could say to her, 'Well, I didn't *lie* to you, I just didn't tell you,' which is a lie by omission. Now that she knows, it's curious. If she had known before, would she have even dated him in the first place? Would she have stayed with him?" Hartley continues, pondering. "It's one of those things where you build this whole relationship, and then you find out the person you're with isn't the person you thought they were. Where does that leave you?"

Hartley took particular pride in his final scene with Lois, where they call off their relationship for good. "Erica and I do good with those, don't we?" he laughs. "I'm pretty happy with the way that we break up. I'm really easy to break up with!"

Erica Durance feels that in addition to not wanting to share Oliver with the rest of the world, Lois wouldn't go back to Oliver because she doesn't want to be hurt again. "You hurt me once, shame on you," Durance says. "You hurt me twice, shame on me, that kind of thing. I think that's how it is, and she just isn't willing to open that door again."

Hartley reveals that 'Siren' was a highlight of his time on *Smallville*. "'Siren' was probably the most fun I've had doing *Smallville*," he says. "When you're new to a show, you just get sucked into the work, which is great, but you don't think about the people you're meeting, because you're meeting them for the first time, and then when you leave, you think you might not see any of them ever again. So coming back was like a reunion. The first thing John Glover said to me as I walked in and I saw him shooting a scene was, 'Welcome home.' I'm really fond of all of those guys. Michael is just so great, I'm a huge fan of his. Tom is wonderful, and has always been

## THE BLACK CANARY

Black Canary may have waited until 2008 to make her first appearance on *Smallville*, but the character has been a major part of the DC Comics universe for over sixty years.

Dinah Lance made her first comic book appearance in 1947's *Flash Comics* #86, wearing her trademark fishnet stockings even in her earliest appearances. The character proved popular and was quickly inducted into the Justice Society of America. When DC revived some of its classic characters in the Silver Age, Black Canary made several guest appearances before becoming a member of the Justice League.

The most famous Black Canary is actually the second heroine to carry the title. It was eventually revealed that the 1940s adventuress was actually the current Black Canary's mother. This second, younger Dinah is the one who had an on-and-off relationship with Oliver Queen in the comics until the characters were finally married in 2007.

Alaina Huffman is not the first actress to play the role in live action. In 1979, an actress known only as Danuta put on the fishnets for the *Legends of Superheroes* TV series, and in 2002, Black Canary made an appearance on The WB's *Birds of Prey* series, where she was played by Lori Loughlin.

Above: Out of costume: Clark Kent and Oliver Queen.

so good to me in every way, and I have a lot of respect for him. I've always had a lot of respect for John Glover. And then I'm really, really fond of Erica, and I got to work with Allison a little bit more this time, which was kind of cool. I really like everybody up there."

## CLARK: I can't tell you the future, Lana. Honestly, I don't know what's going to happen to us, but I promise I'm going to do everything I can to make sure that we can trust each other again. I don't want this to be over.

Another relationship that hit a major turning point in this episode was Clark and Lana's. The couple finally stepped back and were open and honest about what they'd done in the past. Episode writer Kelly Souders explains the rationale behind their confrontation. "We have really reached a point [on the show] where we want more honesty between the characters," she explains, "and one of the things that has kind of funned up the show is that you think of Clark Kent and you think of Lana Lang as these perfect, pure individuals. They're these farm-raised kids who could do no wrong, but over the course of this series, they've actually done these horrific things. It's just that nobody ever brings it to the table. So we wanted them to put down all their armor and be really up front with each other." ■

# FRACTURE

**STORY BY:** Al Septien & Turi Meyer
**TELEPLAY BY:** Caroline Dries
**DIRECTED BY:** James Marshall

**GUEST STARS:** Connor Stanhope (Alexander), Corey Sevier (Finley), Alisen Down (Lillian Luthor), David Patrick Green (Doctor)

Lex and Lois separately track an amnesiac Kara to Detroit, where she has been living for several weeks as a waitress, going by the name Linda. They find Kara locked up by an ex-convict busboy named Finley. Lex and Finley exchange gunshots, and Lex is shot in the head. Finley then locks Lois up with Kara.

Lex is in a coma in the hospital and Clark agrees to use a controversial LuthorCorp project to enter Lex's mind. Clark explores parts of Lex's psyche and learns that Lex's good side — the childlike "Alexander" — is still within him. Clark's exploration inside Lex's mind also shows the darker, evil side of Lex — a side that terrifies Alexander, who is becoming weaker and weaker as time goes on.

Lex begins flatlining, and if he dies while Clark is in his head, both men could perish. Chloe uses her healing powers on Clark and Lex, saving them both but causing her to collapse. Using the address he found in Lex's mind, Clark locates Lois and Kara and saves them from Finley. After Lex recovers, he visits Kara at the Talon and offers to help her with a treatment to regain her memories.

## CLARK (to Alexander): I'll always be there for you.

Michael Rosenbaum enjoyed the chance to once again explore Lex's past during 'Fracture'. "I think that when you're scarred as a child, you tend to lose a lot of memory," he says, "and even when I was a kid, there're things I've forgotten, so I understand that you block dark moments out. The fact that something actually triggers that memory is interesting. Every time they go to a Lex flashback, it's always one of my favorite moments."

Lex using Kara's amnesia to his advantage harks back to a particular season four episode. "You can go back to 'Blank' when Clark got amnesia," points out writer Caroline Dries, "and there's a scene in the library where Lex says, 'Clark, you know you can tell me anything,' and Chloe, knowing Clark can superhear, whispers, 'Be careful, Clark.' Here, Lex is doing the same thing with Kara."

"Kara getting amnesia creates huge stakes for Clark," Dries says, explaining the peril of the situation. "As writers, we're always looking at 'How do we up the ante for Clark?' When his superpowered cousin is thrown into a different city and people are prodding her, it's obviously going to put the attention back on Clark. The second that Lex gets a hold of Kara, it's game on for Clark and his secret."

Kara naively accepts Lex's help at face value. "Kara doesn't really know the type of person Lex is," Laura Vandervoort says. "He comes in like a knight in shining armor, and she thinks he's there to protect her, when really he has ulterior motives."

Opposite: Corey Sevier as Finley.

# FRACTURE

## DID YOU KNOW?

Connor Stanhope returns as young Alexander in the episodes 'Veritas' and 'Descent'.

# FLASHBACK!

*Smallville* has featured flashbacks in many of its episodes. Here's a look at the best of the backward looks that have aired prior to 'Fracture'...

## LINEAGE

Taking a look back at the day after the meteor shower during season two, we see its immediate aftermath, and the deal that Jonathan Kent made with Lionel Luthor to authenticate Clark's adoption...

## RELIC

A generation before Clark Kent met Lana Lang, Clark's father, Jor-El, had a brief romance with a doomed Earth woman named Louise — who happened to be Lana's aunt! It was at this time in season three we saw that Jor-El sending Clark to Kansas was not an accident.

## MEMORIA

A search for lost memory in season three exposes Lex to visions of his brother Julian's death, and Clark "sees" his parents on Krypton for the very first time.

## REUNION

An Excelsior Prep class reunion in season six revisits the beginnings of Lex's conflicts with Oliver Queen.

## PROGENY

In a flashback sequence in this season six episode, we see the day Chloe's mother left her family... and learn that even at the age of twelve, Chloe had an interest in journalism.

## LARA

Glimpses into Kara's past during season seven show her visit to Earth prior to Kal-El's birth, as well as Kara's memories of Clark's mother, Lara. We also see Kara's last moments with her father on Kandor prior to her being sent to Earth.

## SMALLVILLE LEGENDS: THE OLIVER QUEEN CHRONICLES

The origin of Oliver Queen is revealed, and we learn more about the death of his parents and what led him on the path to becoming the Green Arrow. This series served as a prelude to *Justice & Doom*, which more effectively set up the story of the Veritas society.

Playing Alexander was Connor Stanhope. "He was awesome," Dries enthuses. "I liked him a lot. The concept behind him was that any good part of Lex was going to dissolve, and how do we personify the goodness in Lex? We can't just show Lex writing checks to charity anymore. We need to actually show that there's something left for Clark to save. Throughout the series, that has been Clark's mission, to find a way to redeem his mortal enemy. The little boy was a great personification of that."

Above: Inside Lex's mind, Clark sees Lex interacting with "Linda".

## KARA: Clark didn't even mention that you guys were friends. What happened?

Clark's adventure inside Lex's brain must have had an effect on his memories. "When Clark was inside his mind," says Dries, "it was like sifting the dust off things and rattling them up a bit; it stirred all of the memories inside Lex's head."

Allison Mack feels that Chloe using her power to save Lex was right, but that Chloe really did it for Clark. "Chloe would do anything to save Clark," she explains.

Michael Rosenbaum is amused by the number of times his character has been shot. "Lex has to get shot at least three times a year," he says laughing. "And close to death half a dozen times or it's just not a good season. It wasn't my call for him to be shot, and the fact that he was shot in the head and survives... he must have an extra chromosome!"

To double Kara as Linda in the diner, the show's wardrobe crew changed her color palette slightly. "It was very subtle," costume designer Caroline Cranstoun explains. "Kara almost wore her colors — red or blue — but as Linda, she had a more neutral palette. As though her powers were gone and so was her color, and she looked more like the girl next door." ∎

SMALLVILLE MUSIC

'Say It Again' by Marie Digby
'Unease' by Last Page

# HERO

**WRITTEN BY:** Aaron Helbing & Todd Helbing
**DIRECTED BY:** Michael Rohl

**GUEST STARS:** Sam Jones III (Pete Ross), Anna Galvin (Gina), Andrew Fallows (Deejay), Mark Wynn (Lex's Bodyguard), OneRepublic (Themselves)

Trying to reconnect with the still-amnesiac Kara, Jimmy takes her to a local concert for the band OneRepublic. When some scaffolding nearly falls on them, former Smallville resident Pete Ross uses his new stretching powers to save them, the rescue caught on Jimmy's camera.

The now superpowered Pete — who obtained his powers from meteor-enhanced chewing gum — returns to Smallville with a newfound confidence, enjoying the hero worship and even challenging Clark to a game of basketball. He is surprised to see that so much has changed, including all of the people now aware of Clark's powers and Lionel Luthor hanging out in the Kent family kitchen!

Lex threatens Pete and tells him that he will expose Chloe's secret if Pete doesn't steal Kara's bracelet from Lionel's safe. Clark tries stopping him, but Pete immobilizes him with a meteor rock and leaves.

When the time comes for Pete to give Lex the bracelet he refuses, and instead uses his powers to take Lex down. However, his powers begin to fail and Pete is beaten by Lex's henchman. Clark rescues Pete and recovers the bracelet in a blur.

With no more kryptonite-powered gum to give him abilities, Pete returns to normal, but vows to find a way to still be a hero. Meanwhile, Kara visits Lex at the mansion and asks if she can stay with him...

## LEX: However you want to see it, one truth remains: I control Chloe's fate, and if you really want to be her hero, you're gonna put that amazing ability to work for me.

'Hero' featured the long-awaited return of Clark's old friend Pete Ross, who hadn't appeared on the series since the third season episode 'Forsaken'. Michael Rosenbaum was really pleased by the return of his former co-star. "It was surprising — I didn't know if we'd ever see Sam Jones again, or should I say, SJ3," he says with a smile. "It was a pleasant surprise. He's always fun to work with; he has a great energy and is very funny; we have a lot of laughs. If you wanted to know of a place to party in Vancouver, ask Sam Jones!" Bringing back Pete Ross was also good for Rosenbaum's TV alter-ego, Lex. "There's always been this animosity between them," explains Rosenbaum, "from the time Lionel Luthor ruined the Ross family business, and Pete's always blamed Lex, which Lex thought was really unfair. After all the whining and bitching through the years, Lex wanted to use and abuse him, and during this episode he did."

Opposite: Pete Ross is in shock after the discovery of his new powers.

The return of Sam Jones gave Aaron Ashmore a chance to work with someone who for him was a new cast member, as Ashmore didn't join *Smallville* until season six. "I asked Sam what it was like being back," Ashmore recalls, "and he said it felt like nothing had changed. In that respect, he just stepped right back into the role. I liked the dynamic he brought in because he's a nice guy. There is definitely something really cool about him."

Writer Brian Peterson explains that Pete's return provided a useful device to hint at the danger Clark is exposing himself to. "We had reached a point where so many people knew Clark's secret," he says, "that it was a chance for somebody to come back and point out what Clark and a lot of the audience had probably missed, which is that bad things are going to happen. It's only a matter of time. There was actually a part of a scene which was cut from the episode, where Pete very clearly warns Clark that too many people know his secret and something horrible was coming — that was a warning of what would happen in 'Veritas'."

Pete's appearance was also an opportunity for the writers to revisit a character who has left Smallville and Clark Kent behind and examine how all this had affected him. "It was interesting to answer the question of what happens to somebody who knows Clark's secret and has gone away," Darren Swimmer says. "What happens as they live

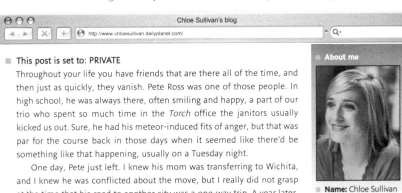

Chloe Sullivan's blog

http://www.chloesullivan.dailyplanet.com/

**This post is set to: PRIVATE**

Throughout your life you have friends that are there all of the time, and then just as quickly, they vanish. Pete Ross was one of those people. In high school, he was always there, often smiling and happy, a part of our trio who spent so much time in the *Torch* office the janitors usually kicked us out. Sure, he had his meteor-induced fits of anger, but that was par for the course back in those days when it seemed like there'd be something like that happening, usually on a Tuesday night.

One day, Pete just left. I knew his mom was transferring to Wichita, and I knew he was conflicted about the move, but I really did not grasp at the time that his road to another city was a one-way trip. A year later, when I found out Clark's secret and learned that Pete knew, I began to understand, but I was still perplexed as to why he never came back.

I shouldn't be surprised that it was the meteors that caused him to drop back into our lives. This time they gave him abilities, and perhaps it was Clark's shadow more than his secret that had kept Pete away all those years. Although the meteor-enhanced Stride Gum that he had been chewing left him with some strange quirks, I could tell once it wore off that the same old Pete was still there — a bit older and more mature, but still the guy I enjoyed tagging along with back in the day.

I know now that even if he's far away, Pete Ross will no longer be a stranger, and he will always look out for me, powers or no. He is a dear friend, and I hope he visits our "leafy little hamlet" more often in the future.

**About me**

**Name:** Chloe Sullivan
**Location:** Metropolis
**Occupation:** Journalist

their lives, knowing that there's somebody like Clark Kent out there? How do they live under that kind of a shadow?"

Above: Laura Vandervoort poses with the band OneRepublic.

Todd Slavkin adds: "The notion of Pete wanting to be a hero is so pure and right for the kid that grew up in Clark Kent's shadow. It was a fun wish fulfillment."

## CHLOE: Chewing gum? Is nothing sacred anymore?

Creator Al Gough is not convinced Pete's visit to Smallville worked for the show. "Poor Pete," he laments, "he can't even headline his own episode! Though I do think it at least gave us some closure to the character."

Many fans objected to the in-your-face appearance of Stride Gum during the episode. "The benefit of product placement is that it allowed us to do some new visual effects," explains Brian Peterson. He also notes that the writers had wanted to do a stretching power episode since the show's first year.

'Hero' marked the end of the brief Kara and Jimmy romance. "It does kind of fizzle," Aaron Ashmore admits. "Chloe is still number one in his mind, and as much as Kara is a sweetheart and so gorgeous, I think there's something about Chloe that Jimmy is really attached to. Plus, when Kara loses her memory, she's got a lot going on, and I think Jimmy's smart enough to know to back off and let her figure things out."

At the end of the episode Kara arrives at the Luthor mansion. Michael Rosenbaum explains why Lex lets her stay. "She has a pretty face, but that's not what it's about for Lex at all — he could have any beautiful woman he wanted. It's all about the truth; it's all about finding out secrets. He's using her, completely. He doesn't want to hurt her, though. He just wants to find out everything she knows." ■

# TRAVELER

**STORY BY:** Al Septien & Turi Meyer
**TELEPLAY BY:** Don Whitehead & Holly Henderson
**DIRECTED BY:** Glen Winter

**GUEST STARS:** Gina Holden (Patricia Swann), Aaron Douglas (Pierce), Anna Galvin (Gina)

Kidnappers wielding kryptonite-powered tasers abduct Clark and place him in a kryptonite-lined cage. Patricia Swann, Dr. Virgil Swann's daughter, accuses Lionel of having the other members of the Veritas society killed. She claims to have proof, which she will release if she is not taken to the "Traveler" — Clark.

Lana and Chloe locate Kara. She and Chloe are then transported to the Fortress of Solitude, where Chloe pleads to Jor-El to restore Kara's powers in order to save Clark.

Patricia Swann demands Lionel introduce her to the Traveler, but Clark's abductor, Pierce, knocks her out. When Lionel tells Pierce to let Clark go, Pierce refuses and then knocks Lionel out. Kara then zooms in and destroys the cage that was holding Clark. Pierce points a gun at Kara and Clark, but Lionel pushes him from the control room and he is then impaled on the wreckage of the cage.

Patricia gives Clark her father's journal, and tells him that the Traveler will bring great change. She also warns Clark to be wary of Lionel. Patricia then returns to Metropolis, where her limo is pulled over and she is shot dead. Her bloodied necklace containing an important key is now in the possession of the man who had her killed — Lex Luthor.

## PATRICIA SWANN: For all the good you do, there will always be darkness.

Setting things up for a darker turn in later episodes, 'Traveler' reignites the question of Lionel's true intentions. "Lionel locks up Clark to keep him out of the way, and safe," writer Don Whitehead explains, "then he keeps him there because Patricia Swann possesses evidence tying Lionel to the Veritas murders. So he is doing the right thing in the wrong way, and then he's doing the wrong thing, but he rationalizes it, which is why he's still the magnificent bastard, but he's trying to fight against his instincts. We're to wonder, if he was really trying to protect Clark, why would he keep him with a jailer like Pierce?

"Here's Lionel, seeing Pierce mess with Clark, yet he keeps him there because he's trying to save his own skin," he continues. "When Lionel tells Clark at the end that he's a changed man, and Clark tells him he isn't and walks away, Glen Winter, the director, came around the back of Lionel, and we stayed with him for a minute, so he's sort of a man alone. As Glen brings the camera around, there's a ceiling lamp above Lionel that, just before the cut, becomes a halo over his head. It's almost like he's the misunderstood saint. Glen Winter, an amazing DP [director of photography], and director, did such a fantastic job with that."

To jumpstart the Veritas storyline, *Smallville*'s writers created Patricia, daughter of Dr.

*Opposite: Virgil Swann's daughter Patricia, played by Gina Holden.*

Virgil Swann. "Christopher Reeve's memorable portrayal of Virgil Swann added so much to *Smallville* that we wanted to call back to his character in a way that did him justice," Whitehead explains. "We needed someone to act as a catalyst for the Veritas/Traveler storyline. Patricia Swann is bright, brave, and good-hearted, like her father. Based on Virgil's research into the Traveler, and the information he has on Lionel and the Veritas murders, Patricia musters her courage and attempts to beat Lionel at his own game. Even though she's out of her element, she believes the stakes are too great, so she marches into the lion's den with her head held high. We can't help but root for her. She hopes to use the murder evidence as leverage to force Lionel to end his relationship with the Traveler. She confronts Lionel and gives Lex his childhood painting of the Veritas symbol so he will put pressure on his father for some answers. She expects Lionel will ultimately make a deal with her in order to keep his past hidden. However, the good in her partially blinds her to Lionel's readiness to play dirty. Her actions fire up Lex more than she realizes. She thinks Lionel is the villain here — she has no idea Lex is now the one who's willing to kill to learn the secret of the Traveler."

The writers were keen to use Patricia to once again touch Clark with his old mentor's wisdom. "Before she dies," says Whitehead, "Patricia's able to fill Clark in on the legend, and shares an important observation — no matter how much good Clark does, there will always

# Daily Planet

### METROPOLIS' GREATEST NEWSPAPER

## PROMINENT CITIZEN DIES UNDER SUSPICIOUS CIRCUMSTANCES

A prominent Metropolis citizen has been found dead in the East Lake near Metropolis. The body of Patricia Swann was discovered floating in the lake this morning by a man walking his dog.

The coroner's report indicates that there may be signs of a struggle, but the exact cause of death has not yet been released to the general public. Metropolis Police are calling for a full and immediate investigation. Swann's purse has not been discovered, so initial suspicion is that a mugging went awry.

Patricia Swann had an education and heart tailored to developing social awareness. She was the daughter of the late Nobel Prize-winning astronomer and 1977 *Time Magazine* Man of the Year Virgil Swann, founder of Swannstar Technologies.

In 2006, Ms. Swann established the Swann House, a complex and assisted living program located in the East Side. Swann House has provided a key role in the development of new and innovative programs across the United States, providiving spiritual care, food services, and social and recreational housing. Swann was also a member of the Board of Directors of the Swann Center, a drug and rehabilitation center based in the Suicide Slums.

Swann graduated from the University of Metropolis with a Master's Degree in Cultural Anthropology, with a minor in Physical Anthropology. In addition to her humanitarian efforts, Swann enjoyed traveling extensively, and had spent three years working on relief programs in South America.

**For more on Swann, see LEGACY | Page A13**

## MUSIC

'Der Holle Rache' by Mozart

Above: Lana and Chloe find the taser darts used to abduct Clark.

be evil. Sometimes Clark needs a reminder that not everything bad that happens is somehow his fault. We specifically wanted to incorporate Virgil Swann into that lesson, so we had Patricia build off a saying she attributes to her father in that scene."

Patricia Swann's sudden death at the end of 'Traveler' was bittersweet for writer Holly Henderson. "On the one hand, her murder was a surprising twist, and beautifully teed up Lex's reckless obsession with uncovering the secret of Veritas. But on the other, I'd love to have seen Virgil's daughter stick around a little while longer. She would have made a wonderful ally and confidant to Clark. We had a pretty clear picture of the type of woman she'd be — a classic beauty, who despite her delicate features, is both strong and determined. We wrote Patricia as if she truly was her father's daughter, both in demeanor and spirit."

## Chloe: I love your son. He's in danger and he needs our help!

Fans of *Smallville* and Chloe in particular enjoyed Chloe's impassioned plea to Jor-El at the Fortress of Solitude. "We know Chloe loves Clark," Whitehead says. "Is it romantic love? Is it platonic love? It's love. It transcends the platonic or romantic... she loves him with every fiber of her being. Here Chloe is willing to face down Jor-El, who can be very dangerous. She's not just saying, 'I love your son, and that's why you should do this,' she's also saying 'Your son is in trouble. You sent him here to Earth to help us, and we need you to help him. I'm here to help him.' She almost becomes an emissary of Kal-El, to come to the father and say, 'Give Kara her powers back to protect your son.' I think Jor-El responds to the fact that his son is being threatened, and sees that right now this is the smartest course of action." ■

# VERITAS

**WRITTEN BY:** Brian Peterson & Kelly Souders

**DIRECTED BY:** James Marshall

**GUEST STARS:** James Marsters (Brainiac), Anna Galvin (Gina), Connor Stanhope (Alexander), Jonathan Scarfe (Robert Queen), Rick Ravanello (Edward Teague), Owen Best (Young Jason Teague), Luke Gair (Young Oliver Queen), Conner Dwelly (Young Patricia Swann), Bud the Dog (Shelby), Michael Denis (Male Nurse), David Lovgren (Lionel's Henchman)

At the Kent farm, Brainiac tries planting ideas in Kara's mind about returning to Krypton. When Clark arrives and recognizes his former foe, Brainiac quickly rockets away. Lex has a flashback to his childhood and remembers a meeting between his father and the other members of Veritas. This memory awakens the knowledge that the society had access to great power, but this power would only be used if the Traveler became a threat. Lex becomes determined to learn this secret. Lex's assistant, Gina, informs him that in order to get access to the vault in Switzerland, he will need another key in addition to the one he obtained after killing Patricia Swann. Lex eventually realizes the remaining key rests with his father.

In another plan to recruit Kara, Brainiac attacks Lana at the Isis Foundation, and when Clark finds her, her eyes are blank. She begins writing a message in Kryptonian, telling him to deliver Kara to the *Daily Planet*. Kara speeds off to the Daily Planet building's roof, where Brainiac says he will restore Lana if Kara comes with him. She agrees. However, Brainiac doesn't keep his word... Lana is still in her catatonic state, and now both Brainiac and Kara are missing.

Lionel visits Chloe at the *Daily Planet* to plead his innocence in the death of Patricia Swann and to warn that Clark is in danger. Chloe says she doesn't believe him and leaves.

## LEX: I've always known my father was covering a secret. A secret of cryptic symbols and mystic stones. I just didn't know it had a name.

Four episodes after returning to power, Brainiac formulated a new plan for achieving his goals. "Brainiac made the mistake the first time around of thinking that Clark was more naïve than he really is," James Marsters says. "He knew that he couldn't really beat Clark in a fight; at best he could hope for a draw. But, he thought, if he used manipulation and lies, then Clark was probably too naïve to catch him. That didn't work. Clark saw through it, so I think Brainiac hoped that Supergirl, being newer to Earth, would be a better target."

Kara's bracelet was also key to Brainiac. "Kara's bracelet is what opened the portal back to Krypton," episode writer Brian Peterson says. "Brainiac needed her bracelet to go through the portal, and so only she could help him get back there."

Opposite: Kara offers herself to Brainiac in order to save Lana.

# WRITERS ON STRIKE

The Writers' Guild of America (WGA) strike was held over a hundred-day period, from November 5, 2007 through February 12, 2008. The strike put hundreds of productions on hold and stopped work on many TV series and movies. The goal of the strike was to achieve gains in several areas for writers, including better deals regarding DVD revenues and "new media", such as streaming video on the Internet. More than 12,000 writers participated in the strike.

Of all of the series on television in the 2007–2008 season, Smallville was one of the most prepared for the strike, with fifteen scripts "in the can" prior to the early November deadline. This kept the Vancouver-based crew in production until late January when 'Veritas' wrapped and the series ran out of scripts.

During the weeks of the strike, the writers frequently picketed and rallied outside the major studios. On Tuesday, November 13, 2007, actors from dozens of television series joined their series' writers to show their support at a rally outside the Universal Studios lot. Joining Smallville's writers were actors Michael Cassidy, John Glover, and Phil Morris. "It was the show-runner/stars day, so all of the stars, show-runners, producers, and writers of various shows choose that day to picket at Universal," Phil Morris recalls. "I called five or six of my friends, and I had a placard where somebody had written Smallville, and I put an apostrophe and an 's' on it, so it read 'Smallville's writers are the real heroes'. It was a great fellowship. I was really honored, because I think that Al and Miles have been very good to me, and I feel like I have been very good to them; none of us can do this by ourselves. Shows are not just improvisational, they are written, they are scripted, and then we go in there and we add our talent to it — but without the writer, without that person or persons scribing these words that we utter, we do not exist, really. I respect those guys and that medium so much. It was my honor to stand in line and support them."

Fans of Smallville also became involved by sending pencils to the studio heads. Of all of the TV series, Smallville was one of the top shows in total volume of pencils ordered. "If we weren't first, we were second," Al Gough notes. "It was a great show of support. Everybody on the staff really appreciated it. The fans have always been great."

At the end the strike, Smallville's writers immediately returned to work, and by mid-March, the Vancouver-based crew was back to work. "We are lucky to be on season seven," writer Holly Harold says. "We're a well-oiled machine, so we actually accomplished quite a few episodes before the strike, and then we were able to pick up where we left off and put together five more episodes after the strike. That is a real tribute to the cast and crew and the whole writing staff, that we were all comfortable enough and confident enough that we could divvy up the workload and just go for it. We came back from the strike in a really good place."

## DID YOU KNOW?

One draft of the 'Veritas' script included Genevieve Teague in the flashback. This was altered to her husband, Edward, when Jane Seymour was unavailable to reprise her role.

Above: Clark and Kara are alarmed by Brainiac's visit to the Kent barn.

Another tool used by Brainiac was the paralysis of Lana as a way to weaken Clark. "Lana is Clark's anchor to humanity," speculates Marsters, "and if Brainiac can get rid of Lana or get her away from Clark, he has a better chance of dehumanizing Clark and having him stop caring so much about the human race."

**CLARK: What did you do to her?**
**BRAINIAC: A little adjustment to her central nervous system. Absolutely irreversible by any human standards, completely reversible by me.**

Lois receives an anonymous tip that Patricia Swann has been murdered, and this sets her off investigating the philanthropist's daughter's death. "The cool thing about 'Veritas' is that everything's building with Lois and her arc of going after the Luthors," Erica Durance says. "She comes across this fantastic story about this murder. There's no way the Luthors are not a part of it, so she decides to go after Lionel Luthor. It's fun to live a little bit in the fabric of the mythology and go after the Luthors, working with Jimmy, and I absolutely loved working with John Glover," she adds.

Aaron Ashmore also enjoyed the opportunity for another Lois and Jimmy team-up.

Above: Brainiac issues an ultimatum.

"I think it's really fun," he says. "Jimmy and Lois are both still working on their investigative skills, and they just barge in on Lionel and confront him with the truth, hoping they will get him to come clean. Lois and Jimmy are a funny pairing because it's almost like a big sister and a little brother. It's a different dynamic than I've been used to with other people."

**LIONEL: (to Lois and Jimmy) Now if that is all from the dynamic duo, security will be happy to help you find your way out.**

Because of the strike by the Writers' Guild of America, 'Veritas' almost became the seventh season finale of *Smallville*. "We usually do three acts to a season," creator Al Gough explains. "And for us, just where the strike was going to fall was going to be 'Veritas', and the plan was to have Lionel's death at the end of that episode as sort of the cliffhanger. Then, when the strike came along, we knew we wanted the end of the season to be Lex discovering what Veritas was hiding — which was Clark — so the plan was that he would get to the Fortress and unlock its secrets. Five or six days before the strike, when we could feel it coming, we went in and raised the cliff and put the whole ending of Lex getting the keys and finding the Fortress as the finale of the episode."

Brian Peterson explains the multitude of elements they were trying to squeeze into this important episode: "'Veritas' was very much one tight story about Lex's quest to get the keys to unlock the secret of the Traveler," he notes, "which was informed by the flashbacks that he had had. So, he killed Lionel on that track. He went to Switzerland, where he found the box, and he eventually ended up at the Fortress of Solitude, all in the same episode. Meanwhile, Brainiac took off with Kara, and Clark was left holding Lana."

Looking back on the conception of the episode, Peterson remembers an early version of 'Veritas' had Brainiac take Kara to the Amazon Rainforest to create her own Fortress of Solitude, within which he could hone his power. "The episode was going to end with Kara hurling her bracelet toward the camera," explains Peterson. "It would have been a homage to the crystal back in the season four finale 'Commencement'." ∎

"Veritas" Episode #15    Carved Swann Crest Concept

Fidelitas

Above: Production art for the Swann family crest.

# Daily Planet

DAILY PLANET

METROPOLIS' GREATEST NEWSPAPER

## QUEEN INDUSTRIES CEO MISSING, PRESUMED DEAD

The booming Metropolis-based Queen Industries confirmed rumors today that their Chief Executive Officer is missing and presumed dead. In a media release, Queen Industries spokesperson Wayne MacLaughlin and Police Chief Sergio O'Shaughnessy confirmed the disappearance of the company's CEO and his wife.

Authorities are remaining tight-lipped over what brought down the Queens' private jet, but details are planned to be released later this week. There were no witnesses to the incident, and flight manifests include seven people aboard the plane, including Robert and Laura Queen. Mysteriously, no bodies have been recovered, and divers from the Coast Guard are continuing their search for clues; however, rough waters and weather conditions have impeded the search thus far.

The Queens' son, Oliver, is safe and has been placed with family members. Shares of Queen Industries stock have gone down by ten points since the original announcement of the CEO's disappearance and possible death.

(Continued On Page A-19)

# DESCENT

**WRITTEN BY:** Holly Henderson & Don Whitehead

**DIRECTED BY:** Ken Horton

**GUEST STARS:** Anna Galvin (Gina), Connor Stanhope (Alexander), Jill Teed (Maggie Sawyer), Don Broatch (Gina's Attacker), Shaw Madson (Lex's Henchman)

Lex has a heated confrontation with Lionel in the hope of obtaining the second key, which he believes will lead him to solve the mystery of the Traveler. When Lionel doesn't comply, Lex pulls a gun on him, then pushes his father out of his office window. Lionel plummets to his doom.

While Lex is questioned by Metropolis authorities, including Maggie Sawyer, he is haunted by visions of his younger self, chastising him for "killing Dad". Unknown to Lex, Jimmy Olsen was taking a photo just as Lionel was about to fall from the high-rise — and the photo reveals that the elder Luthor was indeed pushed.

Lex's assistant, Gina, calms her bereaved boss and he tells her that the key he was seeking is nowhere to be found. Gina then informs Lex that Lionel was seen at the *Daily Planet* the previous night, and Lex eventually learns that Lionel met with Chloe when he was there.

Gina becomes determined to stop any evidence of the truth from surfacing, and when she discovers that Jimmy and Lois have crucial information, she pulls a gun on them and has them locked in the freezer in the *Daily Planet*'s kitchen. They are rescued, but not before the evidence tying Lex to his father's death is destroyed. Gina herself is killed, taken down by an unknown attacker.

Following his father's murder, the good side of Lex represented by his younger self is finally extinguished. Lionel's funeral is a closed service, though Clark pays his respects and silently glares at his former friend, well aware of what he has done.

## LEX: I was raised in your shadow. Now you're going to die in mine.

After seven seasons of friction between Lex and Lionel, things finally come to a dramatic and shocking climax, which Michael Rosenbaum felt had been a long time coming. "I think it stems from the past and the way that Lionel raised Lex, the things he did to him, the mental torture," Rosenbaum explains. "The final straw is when he chooses Clark over his own son. I think Lex feels that he has been betrayed too much, so he had to kill Lionel, for his own sake. He's tried giving his father second chances, but if you watch the show for seven years, you realize that Lex became the way he is because Lionel pushed him to it."

Episode writer Holly Henderson looks back on the complex father-son relationship: "There was a time when Lex feared and admired his father," she notes. "He's spent the better part of his life trying to emulate the man, or at least impress him. Throughout the series, Lex and Lionel's relationship has been a power struggle, a sort of dance, and Lex begrudges the fact that Lionel had the upper hand for so long. Lex grew to define

*Opposite: Lex is haunted by the younger, innocent version of himself after he kills his father.*

# DESCENT

himself by this struggle, to the point that it swallowed up much of his sense of self. Now, one of the few ways he can feel good about himself is by completely overshadowing his father, and you can see where that leads," she smiles.

## LIONEL: In my lifetime, I have known many famous and powerful men. Presidents, sultans, kings... and I believed that I was superior to them all. But I've come to know the truth, Kal-El. My greatest accomplishment is that I have dedicated myself to protecting your life and serving you.

Lex's crime has an almost overwhelming impact on his psyche. "It's one thing for Lex to push Lionel out that window in a moment of passionate anger and resentment, but now Lex has to face what he's done," episode co-writer Don Whitehead points out. "When he identifies his father's body, we glimpse Lionel's bloody eye — and we can imagine what the rest of him must look like. Confronted with the sight of his father's corpse, with what he did to his own father, Lex is shaken to the core, and has something of a psychotic break. He becomes dizzy and disoriented, and just as Lex's childhood memories of Veritas rose up into his consciousness, now little Alexander — his conscience — emerges to challenge Lex with what he's done."

**DAILY PLANET**

http://www.dailyplanet.com/breakingnews

# Daily Planet

METROPOLIS' GREATEST NEWSPAPER

| NEWS | BUSINESS | SPORTS | LIFE & STYLE | |
| WORLD | POLITICS | WEATHER | ENTERTAINMENT | Search: |

**BREAKING NEWS**

## LUTHOR DIES IN FATAL FALL

A well-known Metropolis businessman has been found dead in what police are calling a suicidal jump from a twenty-fifth-story window at LuthorCorp Plaza. The man has been identified and confirmed as LuthorCorp founder Lionel Luthor.

Luthor, who has made Norbes' 100 Wealthiest lists seventeen times since LuthorCorp became incorporated in 1983, was a graduate of Yale with dual Ph.D. degrees in biochemical engineering and macroeconomic modeling. His company raised millions initially in pesticides before expanding into other avenues in recent years.

Funeral arrangements have not yet been announced. Luthor's eldest son, Lex, is expected to make a televised statement on Tuesday.

Related links:
**Luthor Found After Three Months**
**Lionel Luthor Missing**
**Luthor Bride Dies In Explosion**

Above: The former friends pass each other silently at Lionel's grave.

Whitehead was particularly impressed with the director's work in creating this scene. "The way Ken Horton shot it, with the rest of the world swimming around Lex and Alexander, meant we got to experience Lex's state of mind at that moment. Standing off to the side, Clark can see something's up with Lex, something more than grief and mourning. Zeroing in on this, he and Lex eye one another, and then Clark follows Lex — another great Ken Horton moment."

That silent exchange is mirrored at the end of the episode as Clark and Lex stand over Lionel's grave. "There's a beautiful symmetry to those two powerful silent moments, since they bookend the confrontation between Clark and Lex in the mansion, where they argue over their fathers' deaths," Whitehead continues. "Throughout the episode, Lionel's death acts as a catalyst for three iconic Clark-Lex face-offs, each one building in intensity until we see Clark and Lex as the men they will become and the roles they will ultimately play — the hero and the villain.

"I think Lionel proved to Clark that there is redemption for people, even when they're imperfect. Clark at one point wrote Lionel off, and I think Lionel truly surprised him," Whitehead adds. Holly Henderson sees 'Descent' as a chance to answer some of the questions fans have had for many years. "Is Lionel good? Is Lionel bad? What is motivating him? And this was the answer," she notes. "He truly changed by meeting Clark Kent, and was inspired by him, and loved him." ■

# SLEEPER

| WRITTEN BY: Caroline Dries | GUEST STARS: Anne Openshaw (Vanessa Weber), D.J. |
|---|---|
| DIRECTED BY: Whitney Ransick | Rhiannon (Woman at Bar), Don Broatch (Lex's Attacker), Ari Cohen (Regan) |

A woman introduces herself to Jimmy as Vanessa Weber from the Department of Domestic Security. She tells him that Chloe is a threat to national security and demands that Jimmy spy on her or his girlfriend will go to jail. Aware of Chloe's propensity for secrecy, Jimmy feels he has no choice but to comply.

Jimmy snoops around on Chloe's computer and discovers she has been breaking government firewalls. Later, Jimmy tails Chloe at a party held at the Metropolis Satellite Center as she attempts to gain access to a satellite in order to locate Brainiac and Kara. Vanessa locates Chloe at the satellite mainframe and uses violence to try to get answers from her. Jimmy uploads a video game to the mainframe's monitors, distracting Vanessa so he can rescue Chloe. They return to Chloe's loft apartment and discuss what happened, and Jimmy assures Chloe that the government will no longer be coming after them — unknown to her, Lex Luthor has had Chloe's name removed from the government's radar. Jimmy is aware that Lex's "favor" comes at a price.

Meanwhile, new pages are suddenly appearing in Dr. Swann's journals, which leads Clark to believe that they may be clues to finding Brainiac and Kara. With Chloe's help, Clark realizes that they have traveled back to Krypton before it exploded. The only way to find them and to save Lana might be to go back in time...

## CHLOE: You do realize that your greatest superpower is your ability to win me over with just one look, no matter how ridiculous you sound, right?

"We knew we wanted to do a Jimmy Olsen-centric episode," Caroline Dries explains. "We knew that Tom Welling was going to be in prep for [the episode he was directing] 'Apocalypse', so we'd only have him for a few scenes. Ultimately, we decided to do a *True Lies*/*Mr. & Mrs. Smith* kind of thing, which seemed perfect, because it's a concept that we hadn't yet done."

Also key for the episode was to restore the relationship between Jimmy and Chloe. "We wanted to establish that they were back together," Dries notes, "but because of all of the heavy mythology we had coming into this episode, it was really hard to get across that these two have restarted their relationship. We put in that first scene to reset that they are 'Jimmy & Chloe' again, except there's this different feeling, because it's round two [of their relationship]. Chloe now has more secrets than ever because of Clark's Veritas stuff coming to light, so she's keeping another part of Clark's world from Jimmy. For Jimmy we wanted to establish, with him making breakfast and that stuff, that this is

Opposite: Vanessa Weber, played by Anne Openshaw.

Above: Jimmy Olsen to the rescue!

'Mercy' by Duffy
'Dirty Laundry' by Bitter:Sweet
'Shiver' by Madita
'The Beat Is' by Channel Two

still the Jimmy that we know, and so he could have an arc through the episode. Going in, he wasn't keeping any secrets, really, from Chloe."

Dries recalls that not everyone was happy with Jimmy's action man turn. "Aaron Ashmore wanted to be sure that we weren't changing Jimmy too much," she notes, "and I think the writers all agreed that Jimmy is not James Bond, and that's the fun of the episode. The second he goes to Lex, it's like he's back to being Jimmy Olsen. He's being proactive, and he's doing it to protect Chloe, but this is probably the worst thing he can do. Jimmy going to Lex is like making a deal with the devil."

In one scene, Jimmy goes to Clark because he thinks someone close to him has a secret — and Clark's initial reaction is that Jimmy is talking about him. "We love conversations like those because Tom Welling has amazing comedic timing, and so does Aaron Ashmore," Dries says. "It was just fun to have the little beats where Clark thinks the secret is revealed."

Dries sees the tango scene with Jimmy and Chloe dancing as the centerpiece of the episode. "When we broke the episode, throughout the writing process, all I wanted was to make sure we kept that dance scene," she remembers. "When Aaron first read the script, he said to me 'Oh, shoot, I don't know how to dance,' but after doing it, he was like, 'You know what? I knew I had to do it, and I went and owned it.' When I watched the rehearsals, I thought they did such a good job. I thought it was a sort of non-*Smallville* moment that really became a cool *Smallville* moment."

## CHLOE: Why didn't you just come to me, like a normal boyfriend?
## JIMMY: Because a normal boyfriend doesn't get lied to every five minutes by the girl that he thinks he's in love with.

**DID YOU KNOW?**

A scene showing how Lex was able to get back his flight clearance was ultimately cut for time, but the sequence where he learned he was grounded remained, causing some confusion in the final cut.

Creator Al Gough notes that they wanted to suggest that Chloe's many illegal actions could have devastating consequences for her. "There are all of these things that Chloe has done, because she hacks into everything," he says. "The idea is that all of what she's done on behalf of either Clark or the Justice League is finally coming home to roost. Furthermore, it's a card that Lex gets to have on her, and drop on her whenever he wants to — which he does at the end of the season, when Jimmy won't do what he wants."

Chloe's trouble will likely inform her character's arc as the show enters its eighth season. "How many computers can this girl hack into? There's got to be some ramifications," insists Gough. "This really puts Chloe under the gun, and spins her into season eight with, quite frankly, a really big problem." ∎

---

Chloe Sullivan's blog

http://www.chloesullivan.dailyplanet.com/

**This post is set to: PRIVATE**

So... Jimmy Olsen, super spy with the gadgets. Yeah, I didn't believe it either. But, he managed to get me away from a psycho DDS agent, and he assures me that I won't be spending my days in prison, so for that I can be happy.

We still have our secrets. Even with them, I hope we can make things work. Maybe now isn't the time to be in a relationship. I just hope he knows that he is appreciated, even if his pancakes are honestly not the best.

Lana's condition still hasn't improved, though some entries suddenly appearing in Dr. Swann's journal may hold the key to finding Braniac. I look at Clark every day and see the emptiness and confusion associated with not knowing how to help Lana. It hurts. Right now all we can do is hold onto hope that something will come through...

**About me**

**Name:** Chloe Sullivan
**Location:** Metropolis
**Occupation:** Journalist

# APOCALYPSE

**WRITTEN BY:** Al Septien & Turi Meyer
**DIRECTED BY:** Tom Welling

**GUEST STARS:** James Marsters (Brainiac), Camille Mitchell (Nancy Adams), Brett Dier (Blond Clark Kent), Carlo Marks (George Dean), Terence Stamp (Voice of Jor-El)

As Clark debates traveling back in time to save Kara on Krypton, Jor-El transports him to different plane of existence to see how things would have been had he never made it to Earth. In this other place, Jonathan Kent and Sheriff Adams are both alive, Chloe has a fiancée, Lana is married and living in Paris, and Lois is a Pulitzer Prize-winning reporter. Lex Luthor's fate is also quite different: he is President of the United States, with Kara by his side as Linda Danvers, and Milton Fine pulling the strings behind the scenes, leading the world toward nuclear war. Clark enlists Kara's help in explaining to Lex that he is being manipulated, but instead finds that Lex knows exactly what he's doing. Lex shoots Clark with kryptonite bullets and has Kara taken away in kryptonite handcuffs. Brainiac prepares to shoot Clark and tells him how he plans to release Zod from the Phantom Zone and create a new Krypton. Brainiac fires the gun and Clark… awakens in the real world.

Clark's vision convinces him that he must return to Krypton to stop Brainiac and save Kara. Together Kara and Clark defeat and destroy Brainiac and save baby Kal-El. Upon returning home, they discover that stopping Brainiac hasn't woken Lana from her comatose state, and unknown to Clark, Kara is in excruciating pain…

## LOIS: Kent, this is no time to be modest. Armageddon's minutes away.

'Apocalypse' was the third episode of the series to be directed by the show's star Tom Welling. "Tom did a wonderful job directing," episode writer Turi Meyer notes. "He was really into the script and where the journey took him in the episode. He knew where he wanted to be and what he wanted to do, and I think the episode benefits from that."

"It's a really tough thing to pull off," Meyer's co-writer Al Septien adds, noting the difficulty for an actor of performing in an episode as well as directing it. "Tom has pulled it off three times expertly, and this episode was particularly tough because it's a very linear, Clark-centric story. Usually our show has an A and a B plot, or sometimes an A, B, and a C plot. This is one plot, from beginning to end, and Clark is in every scene but two. There are short clips at the middle and end of the episode, and there is one two-person scene that he's not in. Every other scene, Clark Kent is there. Tom did a yeoman job of directing an episode with that kind of setup. It was very tough."

Turi Meyer went to the Vancouver set as 'Apocalypse' was shooting and saw Welling in action. "It was inspiring, being there and seeing him work," he enthuses. "He really brought his A game, and he was just dead on in every take. He was great."

Opposite: Clark Kent goes undercover as a mild-mannered reporter for a great metropolitan newspaper.

**SMALLVILLE MUSIC**

'Fetish' by Redana and M1

The decision to show Clark in his iconic suit-and-glasses look came at the suggestion of Al Gough. "When we were breaking the episode, Al Gough told us that he'd really like to see the iconic Clark and the iconic Lex, since it was the 150th episode," Turi Meyer reveals. "We had to come up with a story where we were able to use both of those, and this story lends itself really well to it. We got the extra bonus of Lois dressing Clark in his iconic Clark Kent get-up."

### CLARK: There's still time. I have to make it right. I have to go to Krypton.

Lex and Clark were not the only characters sporting their iconic looks, as Meyer points out. "In the *Daily Planet* you've got Jimmy in the bow tie, snapping pictures, and then Lois being what we know from the mythology was just a gas to write."

Al Septien adds that playing with the Clark and Lois classic relationship was a treat for the writers. "It also allowed us — because it's an alternate reality — to be able to take Clark and Lois from the first time they met through to where their relationship is in the later comics," he says. "She does find out his powers. She goes from bumping into this 'bumbling guy' at the *Daily Planet* to realizing he's a super hero."

Meyer credits the chemistry between Tom Welling and Erica Durance as a high point of the episode. "They're a lot of fun to watch," he says. "Any episode where they have a scene together, there's a lot of chemistry, and in this one, I think they were also enjoying the iconic side of it all, which [normally] we can't do."

The alternate reality also offered the episode's writers a chance to bring back a fan-favorite character from the series' past. "Of all of the characters that we've had in the series, we have a soft spot in our hearts for Sheriff Adams," Meyer reveals, explaining the

## SMALLVILLE LEGENDS: KARA AND THE CHRONICLES OF KRYPTON

Similar in nature to the previous year's *Smallville Legends: The Oliver Queen Chronicles*, *Kara and the Chronicles of Krypton* was the second animated offering tying into the show. Unlike the previous series, *Kara* had a more traditional animated style. The six-part series explored Kara's last days on the planet Krypton and offered new revelations about Zor-El and his connection to Zod and the planet's destruction.

The shorts were originally released as exclusives on Sprint phones before being posted on CWTV.com. All six mobisodes can also be found on the *Smallville: The Complete Seventh Season* DVD set.

**DID YOU KNOW?**

Linda Danvers was the name of Kara/Supergirl's alter ego in many DC Comics stories.

Above: President Luthor, with Milton Fine at his side.

decision to have her return as Lois's informant in the alternate world. Also alive in the other reality was Jonathan Kent, though *Smallville* did not approach John Schneider to return. "There was a temptation, but I think we all realized that would probably be impossible to make it happen," Meyer confirms.

In this altered world, Clark found that he had been replaced in the lives of some of those special to him. The Kents have a son of their own, and Chloe has a fiancée. "In this reality, Chloe ends up with a guy who is similar to Clark, and they're getting married and things are good for her," Meyer notes. "We cast someone with a certain look that mirrored Clark." At first glance, it seemed that everyone was better off without Clark — until the real circumstances of this world were revealed. "Eventually, when Clark realizes Lois is getting arrested, and that somehow Kara is arresting her, and Lex is president, everything hits the fan," explains Septien, "and from there on out it's a nightmare."

The episode also explored the idea of what would have happened if Kara had been found and adopted by the Luthors. "I thought Laura did a great job in the episode," Meyer says. "She was strong; she was forceful. It was a good episode for her."

At the end of the show, Kara is shown to be in pain, foreshadowing revelations two episodes later in the season finale. "We wanted people to think that Kara had destroyed Brainiac," Meyer notes, "and then, when they go back to the future, you realize something is wrong." Septien adds, "But, by the end of the season, you find out that in fact, Kara is not Kara." ∎

## DID YOU KNOW?

In the alternate world, Lana was married to a man named Pierre Rousseau. In the comic books, Lana ended up being married to the similarly named Pete Ross.

# QUEST

**WRITTEN BY:** Holly Harold
**DIRECTED BY:** Ken Biller

**GUEST STARS:** Robert Picardo (Edward Teague), Donnelly Rhodes (Milosh Novak), Ari Cohen (Regan), Sarah Hayward (Guard), James Rowley (Guard), Don Broach (Lex's Attacker), Patrick Sabongui (Agent)

**DID YOU KNOW?**

Only four of season seven's eight series regulars appeared in this episode.

As Lex continues on his quest to learn the secrets of the Traveler, a cloaked stranger attacks him and carves into his chest Kryptonian symbols that form a special message. The symbols lead Clark to St. Christopher's Cathedral in Montreal, Canada, where he meets Edward Teague, the sole survivor of the Veritas clan. When it appears that Clark does not want to fulfill his destiny, Teague immobilizes him and straps him to an altar laced with liquid kryptonite, sacrificing Clark so that no one can have the means to control him. Chloe arrives in Montreal using Oliver's jet and frees Clark before he is sacrificed.

Lex arrives at the cathedral and places the cryptograph inside a clock, and a Scottish melody begins playing. With that clue, Lex heads for Scotland before realizing that the melody was a clue referring to his own mansion. There, he locates the final item — an orb that reveals to him the location of the Fortress of Solitude.

## EDWARD TEAGUE: Lex Luthor cannot be allowed to control you. No one can!

"When we laid down the groundwork for 'Veritas', we wondered what would happen if someone had survived, and every now and then someone would ask what had happened to Edward Teague," episode writer Holly Harold explains. "Jason and Genevieve Teague had died, but he was out there. It was fun to bring him back for 'Quest'."

To catch Clark's attention, a carving with a Kryptonian message was etched into Lex Luthor's chest. "We wanted something that would leap out at the viewer," explains Harold, "and we also wanted something that would call out to Clark, but also serve as a warning. That was really tough, because everybody wondered at its purpose, and who was supposed to see it. Is it a message? Is it not? It was both a warning, and a message, to see if the Traveler is there. I found writing the brutal scenes and then seeing it happen was a lot of fun."

The intricate pursuit of clues and division of the elements that ultimately control the Traveler was Dr. Swann's doing. "Swann was an idealist," Harold notes. "He doesn't want to believe that Clark could ever go bad or that something could happen to him, but he had impressed on him by Jor-El the importance of a safeguard. So, by necessity, and out of protection for the Traveler, he divided up the information and the ability to access it."

Lex's pursuit of this information dominated this half of the season. "Lex knowing that he is about to discover everything is the driving force behind this run of the series," Harold says. "His whole life was secondary to his father's main purpose, and now, to be able to find out why, and to have all of his suspicions proven... he's fanatic about it."

In this episode Jimmy started to learn more about the symbols that had been seen around Smallville for centuries. "I just love that Jimmy, in his innocence, stumbled onto something

Opposite: The lone survivor of the Veritas society — Edward Teague (Robert Picardo).

Above: Teague weakens Clark to prepare him to be sacrificed.

that's been the crux of our series ever since season two," Harold says with a smile. "Using Jimmy was a way to bring in a fresh voice, putting him on a trail that, inevitably, anyone with a curiosity in Smallville is going to hit upon."

**CLARK: As long as there's something out there that can control me, I'm still a threat, and Teague reminded me how dangerous my abilities are. In the wrong hands, Chloe, they can destroy everything.**

Robert Picardo of *Star Trek: Voyager* fame was chosen to play the last member of Veritas. "We've always enjoyed Robert Picardo's characters," Don Whitehead says, speaking for Holly Henderson and himself. "The Doctor was one of the best characters on *Star Trek: Voyager*, and he plays a fantastic thorn in everyone's side as Richard Woolsey on the *Stargate* series. Woolsey's strong sense of decency and obsession with the letter of the law is what makes him such a great foil at times, and an ally at others. Edward Teague also has a passionate obsession that makes him a strong ally and a dangerous enemy. In fact, when Clark meets him, Teague has become a zealot. At first he seems steadfast in his belief that the Traveler will save mankind. However, Teague quickly turns on Clark because his faith came from a place of fear. Mr. Picardo does a tremendous job of portraying characters who at first seem set in their sense of action and purpose, and then revealing the more complex man beneath the surface."

Directing 'Quest' was Ken Biller, also a *Star Trek: Voyager* veteran who had not directed *Smallville* since the third season. "Ken is a really wonderful director," Holly Harold notes. "He wrote and directed season three's 'Shattered', which was amazing, so that had been in Al and Miles' heads for a while. It was great to have him back, and he did a fantastic job." ■

# THE VERITAS SOCIETY

Edward Teague was the last surviving member of the Veritas society. Here are some of the other known members of the elite clan...

## VIRGIL SWANN
Dr. Virgil Swann was a scientist specializing in satellite communications. In 1989, Swann intercepted a communication from Krypton announcing the arrival of Kal-El. Swann was killed two years after first making personal contact with Clark. Swann had a daughter, Patricia, who shared some of his personal journals with Clark before her own death.

## ROBERT & LAURA QUEEN
Robert Queen, father of Oliver, was one of Dr. Swann's closest confidantes and didn't agree with Lionel Luthor's plans to control the Traveler. Shortly before the Traveler's planned arrival, Lionel arranged for Queen and his wife to be killed in a plane crash.

## GENEVIEVE TEAGUE
Edward's wife, and a descendant of the Duchess Gertrude, Genevieve's goals mostly revolved around getting a hold of the three Stones of Power for herself. Lana killed her when she was possessed by the witch Isobel Thoreaux.

## LIONEL LUTHOR
Knowing of the Traveler's pending arrival, Lionel purposely arranged to be in Smallville at the time of the meteor shower. His views and desire to control the Traveler put him at odds with the other members of the organization. In learning more about the Traveler, and getting to know and protect him as Clark, Lionel finally found redemption. For a short time, Lionel even served as the vessel of Jor-El.

## BRIDGETTE CROSBY
Bridgette Crosby was Dr. Swann's emissary, and they had a relationship at one time. It is unknown what Crosby's involvement was in Veritas. Soon after Dr. Swann's death, Crosby herself was killed by Jason and Genevieve Teague, who were after the Water element.

# ARCTIC

**WRITTEN BY:** Don Whitehead & Holly Henderson
**DIRECTED BY:** Todd Slavkin

**GUEST STARS:** James Marsters (Brainiac), Robert Picardo (Edward Teague), Julie Anderson (Nurse), Adam Lolacher (Agent), Ari Cohen (Regan)

Posing as Kara, Brainiac attacks Edward Teague in a private jet and demands to know where to find the device that controls the Traveler. Teague tells her Lex Luthor might know, and she flies off, leaving the plane to crash. Studying the black box audio recording from the plane, Chloe and Clark discover Kara's connection to the attack. Chloe lures Kara to the Talon and tries to incapacitate her with kryptonite. Brainiac's true form is revealed, and he attacks Chloe. Her powers save her from death and weaken Brainiac.

Clark battles and defeats Brainiac, finally freeing Lana from her coma — though unknown to Clark, Kara is trapped in the Phantom Zone. Clark gets to the hospital only to find that Lana has left a video message telling him not to follow her. Chloe also leaves the hospital fully recovered — and is arrested by the Department of Domestic Security.

Clark travels to the Arctic for his final confrontation with Lex. When Lex puts the Kryptonian orb into its final position in order to control the Traveler, the Fortress begins to collapse on top of both of them.

## LEX: I love you like a brother, Clark. But it has to end this way.

Brainiac masquerading as Kara echoed Bizarro's impersonation of Clark at the start of the season and also helped Brainiac toward his endgame. Holly Henderson explains Brainiac's unfulfilled plan. "Brainiac can't touch the crystal, and he wants to control Clark, so he's going to lead Lex to the Fortress," she notes. "His idea is that when Lex puts the crystal into the console, Brainiac's going to somehow maneuver it so he has the power."

Henderson's co-writer Don Whitehead adds: "In 'Apocalypse', we see Brainiac working for Lex Luthor. In a way, that could become their relationship — if everything went according to Brainiac's plan. He can manipulate Lex as Lex manipulates the Traveler."

'Arctic' saw the conclusion of Clark and Lana's romance — with a video message from Lana saying her goodbyes. "She knew if she saw him, she would never be able to leave," Brian Peterson says. Darren Swimmer adds, "Her primary concern is Clark's wellbeing, and she knew that it was in Clark's best interest that she not be a part of his life anymore."

As Kristin Kreuk was still in Thailand shooting the movie *Street Fighter: The Legend of Chun-Li*, *Smallville* sent James Marshall's assistant, Christopher "Tucky" Petry, to film Lana's video. Following the episode's airing some fans expressed their disappointment at the video message on message boards. Director Todd Slavkin admits that it was not an ideal way for the show's most popular couple to break up. "It was a pity that it was a Dear John video," he says. "Fortunately, Kristin was gracious enough to let us send someone over to Thailand and shoot her, and she did an awesome job."

Opposite: Clark's conflict with Brainiac leads to a shocking season finale.

Above: After seven seasons, Lex *finally* learns the truth...

"We were lucky to have the video," Brian Peterson reveals. "At one point, it was going to be a letter, because we just didn't have Kristin." Kelly Souders adds, "We were just thrilled to have *anything*, because it felt strange not to have any presence of Lana in the finale."

## LANA: I need you... but the world needs you more.

If losing Lana would force a major change in Clark's life, the final sequences for Lex had to be just as big. "We knew we needed to have a mythic moment of Lex finding the Fortress," Al Gough explains. "With him discovering Clark's secret, and realizing that everything his father had done, the culmination of seven years, has come down to this. For Miles and I, it's not the ending we envisioned for the series, but it certainly gave closure to these seven seasons. These guys started out as friends. Now Lex has crossed way over to the dark side, and Clark has to really assume his mantle. Now they're finally having a face-off, and in a true *Smallville* fashion, it's not ending well for Clark."

Don Whitehead agrees this was a huge moment. "Lex has always suspected something was off with Clark, and we've watched their relationship sour over for a long time," he notes. "Lex, all along, has just wanted to know the truth. That's all he's been looking for, and Clark has been lying to him for so long. The thing is: how could Clark ever tell somebody like Lex Luthor the truth, when we know what Lex does once he knows the truth?"

Clark and Lex's complex relationship is unraveled in this final face-off. "Here are two men locked in this terrible, grim struggle," Whitehead notes. "Finally, all bets are off. Clark realizes Lex now knows he is the Traveler. Lex is deeply, deeply hurt, yet he still sees Clark

'Enough' by Homy
'Perfect' by Michelle Featherstone

as a brother. Lex wants to be the one to save the world. He is going to plunge that crystal home for two reasons. One is to subdue the threat of the Traveler; the other is a payback. He's feeling hurt by Clark. That's why Lex is thinking they're going to go out together."

The episode's director, Todd Slavkin, says that Michael Rosenbaum's final scenes on the show were very emotional to shoot. "It was a fifteen-hour day on the Fortress of Solitude set," he says. "Michael bought a thousand dollars' worth of sushi for the entire crew, and he was bigger than life. He's always a presence on the set, but imagine him being center stage, holding court. There's this great moment on the last shot when he looks right into the camera and he's like 'Goodbye, Smallville.' You could see him getting emotional, and he and Tom hugged. For the whole crew — these people have spent the last seven years with him — it was a big goodbye." He adds, "I live in LA, so I'm going to see Michael, and the four of us are always going to be in contact. He's become a friend. But it was tough." ■

*Shortly before 'Arctic' aired, Michael Rosenbaum announced that season seven would be his last for the show. In this letter, Michael says goodbye to his fans...*

Dear *Smallville* Fans,

Well, it's been seven wonderful years. Your support is what has made *Smallville* so successful, and I appreciate you all more than you know.

That being said, it is time for me to start the next chapter of my life and career. I hope that I gave you some enjoyment over the years, and that you found my portrayal of Lex Luthor to be satisfying. I am truly grateful, as *Smallville* fans are the best fans out there. I sincerely hope that you will continue to follow my career through my hair growth period and beyond.

I'm very excited about what the future holds, but certainly, *Smallville* will always be a part of me. I will definitely miss the greatest crew in the world, and the wonderful cast that has been like a family to me.

Thank you Al and Miles for creating the show. Thank you writers, producers, directors and editors. Thanks Tollin, Robbins and Davola for being there for the pilot. Thank you Peter Roth for employing me for ten years. Lisa Lewis, I miss you already. John Glover, thanks for helping me feel more comfortable touching other actors while acting. Bizarre, but helpful.

Mostly, I want to thank Greg Beeman for directing the "Oh, Sherry" video, by Steve Perry, back in the eighties.

Thanks crew. Thanks fans. Thanks *Smallville*.

I love you all,
Michael Rosenbaum

# CLARK KENT

## "Trust me, Lex. There's nothing that's lost that can't be found again."

Season seven of *Smallville* was described by the show's executive producers as a "loss of innocence" for Clark Kent. The season was full of ups and downs for the character, from learning more about his origins through newly-arrived family members; discovering a secret society that revolves solely around him; facing a bizarrely evil mirror image in Bizarro; losing a mentor in Lionel; to losing Lana, getting her back, and losing her all over again. These adventures climaxed in what may be the show's final showdown between Clark and his nemesis Lex Luthor.

As the season began, it seemed that Clark's love, Lana, had died, and according to the show's producers, that unleashed a new determination and direction in Clark. "When he believed that Lana was dead, it brought out Clark's true feelings about Lex, which he constantly covers up because he doesn't want to think bad things of anyone, especially someone who had been such a close friend," Kelly Souders explains. "One of the things that Lana's death did was bring those feelings to a head, and some real honesty came out between the two of them."

Before Clark finds out that Lana is in fact still alive, he had to stop his genetic duplicate, Bizarro. Tom Welling played the villain in a dual role. "I think it's a testament to Tom's acting skills that he's able to pull off two completely different personalities. It was very impressive," Souders notes. Brian Peterson agrees. "Whenever you do a personality change, you want to make sure that it's going to be convincing," he adds. "If you go all the way back to [season four's] 'Transference', when he was playing Lionel Luthor, that was a good indication of the kind of performance he was going to give as Bizarro. He gave an amazing performance then, and he did a great job with Bizarro as well."

"It's a challenge to pull off this 'anti' version of a character you do all the time," Souders continues. "It's not easy to figure out how Bizarro should act when you're playing Clark Kent. You want there to be some similarities since they're inhabiting the same persona on some levels; but, on the other hand, they're opposites and extremes. Tom did a great job with inventing his own version of Bizarro."

"I think he's disgusted by it," Todd Slavkin says of Clark's reaction to his double. "I think there's part of him that is repulsed by that kind of behavior. Though I think there's also a part of him that admires Bizarro and wishes that he could be as fearless and as passionate as he is, and as honest as he is, because Bizarro doesn't lie like Clark Kent lies."

"I think that's reflected in Lana's reaction later in the season, because Lana actually fell for Bizarro," Brian Peterson points out. "There were parts of Bizarro that Lana loved more than Clark, so there's no way for Clark *not* to be jealous of that kind of honesty."

Introducing Clark's Kryptonian cousin Kara gave the character more of a look into his origins, as well as some much-needed family. "With Kara, we definitely got to explore Clark's back story on Krypton and the story of his family," notes Peterson. "We

Above: Kara's appearance allowed Clark to learn more about his Kryptonian heritage, including his mother, Lara.

had never really had anyone to help voice all the things that he had been feeling about returning to Krypton. He wanted to see his family and his birth parents; but he's cut all of that off, and Kara brought those emotions to the forefront."

Darren Swimmer does not believe that Kara being able to fly diminished Clark's character at all. "I think if anything it accentuated the idea that Superman is more than just his abilities," he states. "It's his strength of character and his heroism. Although Kara had more physical tricks up her sleeve, she hadn't had the growth and the character and the maturity that Clark has now."

Kara's appearance presented the opportunity to explore the House of El for the first time, and through Kryptonian science, Clark was able to interact with a facsimile of his biological mother, Lara. He also faced affirmation that there was evil on Krypton — as evidenced by Brainiac and Kara's father Zor-El — and he would again suffer the punishment of his father Jor-El, who imprisoned him in the Fortress of Solitude for several weeks for disobeying his orders. In further drama, this season he saw his friend Chloe cope with being among the meteor-infected, and witnessed Lex's descent into evil, destroying all that was good inside him.

The arrival of Patricia Swann and Clark's imprisonment within a kryptonite cage left a permanent mark on Clark — who, in addition to learning about a secret organization dedicated to studying the Traveler, would also see Lionel killed by his own son. "It was a tragedy for Clark, that he didn't believe Lionel up until the last second," Kelly Souders says. "For him, it was a regret, looking back at the person who turned out to be finally helping him, and Clark didn't believe him."

"As Chloe pointed out in 'Quest', Clark's going to be playing God for the rest of his life and making choices that a normal human can't, so he's going to have to embrace that," Brian Peterson says. "He's going to have to embrace his destiny sooner or later, and he's just one step closer to that."

Season seven finally gave Clark and Lana their chance at a relationship — however, this comes to a tragic end when Brainiac attacks Lana, placing her in a coma. When Brainiac is defeated and Lana awakens, Clark knows not to go after her, even if he could make his search at superspeed. "She tells him, 'Please don't come looking for me,' and he understands what that meant. It would be bad for both of them," Todd Slavkin notes.

Phil Morris, who played John Jones in two episodes of season seven, is thankful for the time he is able to spend working with Welling. "It's wonderful that I get a chance to work with Tom," he enthuses. "He's humble. We speak about everything from life to

martial arts — the works, and I find that to be a very refreshing place to be, [especially] with somebody you're working that intensely with."

Being a clued-up comics fan, Phil Morris often finds Welling picking his brain on Superman mythology. "Tom's not a huge fan of comics — he's not *not* a fan; he's just not a *big* fan of them," notes Morris. "He doesn't know all of the things that I know. So, in a way, I was coming to Tom with all of this knowledge that is kind of like the knowledge John comes to Clark with! He said to me, 'I didn't know that you're like the second-most powerful character to Superman. You and another guy.' I said, 'Shazam!?' He goes, 'Right! That guy!' And I said, 'You and me' — and I even said 'you and me,' not 'Superman and John Jones.' — 'You and me and Shazam! are the three most powerful beings aside from Darkseid, probably in the DC Universe.' So I bring him interesting information. We talk about acting, we talk about martial arts — I've been taking kung fu for twenty years. He's really interested in that kind of combative training. It's great to just talk to him as a regular guy, and I think it lends to our relationship on-screen. That's what I see in it, and I think that's what the audience sees as well.

"I think Clark was so well cast," Morris adds. "They found a very wholesome guy with a very winning, very fresh kind of personality, and he has taken this character and done incredible work with him. I'm proud to call Tom Welling a friend of mine. I look forward to the next time I work with him." ∎

Above: Before her death, Patricia Swann gave Clark her father's journals.

# LANA LANG

"Clark, I just want to grab onto you and never let you go. But one day the world will need you more than I do, and I don't want to be the one holding you here."

When Lana was last seen in season six, she appeared to have died in a fiery explosion right after telling Lex she was leaving him. In actuality, Lana had faked her death and it was an inactive clone in her vehicle. The real Lana went into hiding in Shanghai, although her disappearance didn't last for long and she found herself back in Smallville within a matter of weeks. Upon her return, Lana was finally let in on Clark's secret, but secrets of her own, combined with the events of the past two years, greatly altered their dynamic. "In the early episodes of the season, Clark was dealing with the fact that she had married Lex and slept with Lex," Al Septien explains. "He loved her and wanted to take care of her, and he was very happy that she came back into his life, but it was a very human thing to be somewhat detached from a person who, for the previous year, had shown him a side of herself that he had never seen before."

Unknown to Clark, Lana was in fact doing some things that could be seen as typical of her former name of Luthor. "I think she was purely 'a woman scorned'," Al Septien explains. "Lex did horrible things to her, and she's out to destroy him in any way that she can. He made her think that she was pregnant so that she would marry him, and she comes out of that scarred. What she wants first and foremost is revenge, so the season starts off there, and as it progresses, she realizes that that's the wrong thing."

Lana's activities included hiring a crazed woman named Marilyn to keep Lionel Luthor captive in a cabin near Reeves Dam. Lionel eventually escaped but Lana's behavior surprised him. "It just gave Lionel a little bit more respect for Lana, because he realized that she's capable of thinking the way he does," John Glover recalls.

Lana's dark side comes to a head in 'Wrath', when a superpowered Lana uses her new abilities to go after Lex. "By the end of 'Wrath', I think she learns that she's got to put that behind her and just continue with her own life," notes Septien. "But for the first half of the season, she was out for blood, and she doesn't want to show Clark that side of her."

Not all of Lana's deeds in the first half of the season had bad intentions. Very early on, Lana put the money she was awarded in her settlement from Lex toward building the Isis Foundation. Although the foundation was partly a front for Lana's spying on Lex, she also did genuinely want to help people. "Lana's initial intention [with Isis] was to help meteor freaks," Todd Slavkin explains. "In one episode, there's a scene where Chloe goes there, and Lana has some people in a waiting room."

"Lana helped a lot of people that we didn't see on-screen," Darren Swimmer adds. "All of the settlement money that she got from Lex was put to good use."

Above: The acquisition of Clark's powers sent an angry Lana on a violent rampage.

Lana's relationship with Clark suffered further damage when it was discovered that the Clark who had become more accepting of her, who was telling her all of the things that she wanted to hear, was actually his genetic duplicate, Bizarro. Despite this revelation, Clark and Lana still tried to continue as a couple, even opening up to one another about past transgressions.

Kristin Kreuk missed the final five episodes of season seven, as she was in Thailand playing the titular role in the film, *Street Fighter: The Legend of Chun-Li*. "Kristin's manager came to us during the writers' strike and told us that Kristin had the opportunity to do the *Street Fighter* movie, but it would require her being gone for a certain amount of time," Al Gough reveals. "We didn't know when the strike was going to end, and at that point, it looked like it was going to drag on for a long time, so we said it was fine for her to do the movie. We already had an ending for the season for Lana, with her being in the coma, so it was all right."

The *Smallville* creators *did* drive a bit of a hard bargain, though. "We made a deal so that if the strike did end, we could write her out of that arc of the episodes," says Gough, "but they'd have to allow us to show her image, or clips. We also made a deal that if we let her out of some episodes, we could have her for some of season eight."

"We've always wanted to give the actors on our show the opportunity to do movies or, in John Glover's case, Broadway plays and things like that, and this way at least Lana will be in the eighth season," Gough adds, pointing out that Kristin Kreuk was only contracted for the first seven seasons of the series.

Kristin Kreuk did film one last season seven appearance — a video in which Lana tells Clark that she is moving on, and that he shouldn't try to find her. Examining the reasons for Lana's departure, Holly Harold says, "Keep in mind, Lana was aware of everything during the coma. Brainiac said she knows everything that's going on around her. So, all those times that Clark is talking to her and she can't respond — she knows what this is doing to him, and she knows that Brainiac came after her to get at Clark. It's not so much 'Peace out, Clark', it's more like, 'I am your biggest weakness, and I'm going to step aside so that it can't happen to you again.' Which is, to me, heartbreakingly noble, and that kind of selfless giving is very rare and really admirable."

Harold also feels both the men in Lana's life have lied to her and caused her pain, all of which contributed to her decision to leave Smallville. "Lana has been really damaged from her time with Lex, and I think also from all the years that Clark lied to her. It's impossible to have a relationship with someone who is not honest with you, and

Clark wasn't. As much as he professed his love to her, he didn't tell her who he really was. So that means you're starting out on some very unstable ground, with that lack of trust — and Lex showed her a darkness in herself. She saw things she was capable of that she may never be able to buy back. That's been her rollercoaster all the way up to, 'This relationship is going to work. I know who Clark is now. I can do this.' And then, of course, Brainiac showing her that in fact, 'It's better that you don't.' It's tragic."

Holly Henderson adds, "I feel like from the beginning of this season we knew that this was going to be the end of their romantic relationship."

Turi Meyer also feels that their separation was inevitable. "By the end of season six she knew who Clark was, and she accepted him and loved him and wanted to be with him for the rest of her life," he says, "and I think she started out this season hoping that that was possible. She gave him up last year, when she faked her death and went to China, but after all of that, she came back and was willing to finally give it a go. They're together, and by the end of the season, what she realizes is: she can't. It's the same tragic realization that Clark has had, which is: this can never be. There is something bigger than the two of them at work, and she has to let him go. Lana has become the tragic figure from the comic books." ▪

Above: Although Lana's secrets — particularly concerning the Isis Foundation — caused conflict between her and Chloe, the two women worked together to rescue Clark.

# LEX LUTHOR

## "You'll never threaten the world again... Kal-El."

Season seven started for Lex with a scene that echoed *Smallville*'s very first episode — an underwater rescue. Instead of Clark, this time it's Kara who comes to Lex's aid, and her presence arouses Lex's curiosity early in the season. "All of his suspicions are starting to be founded," notes Holly Harold, "and just having seen her in the water, that vision of an angel, he wonders where exactly she came from. He's suspicious by nature, and now he's got a target for that suspicion."

Also plaguing Lex at the start of the season is the apparent death of his wife, Lana Lang. Lex doesn't believe she's really dead and eventually discovers her alive and well in Shanghai. Having found her, Lex does something surprising – he seemingly lets her get away with her deception. "It's not to say that Lex would ever let anybody get away with anything," Michael Rosenbaum says. "Maybe he truly loved Lana, so he's letting her go as much as he can, or maybe he has ulterior motives. Obviously he's got other things on his agenda, so maybe it's all about what's more important, and that's not at the top of the list."

As the season progresses, Lex becomes a master manipulator, with Grant Gabriel, Black Canary, Pete Ross, and even Jimmy Olsen all doing his bidding. "Lex is very smart; he's very meticulous," explains Rosenbaum. "He knows what turns people, and how to make them do what he wants, and that's a gift — I know he goes about it the wrong way, but that's what happens sometimes. When people don't cooperate, they get hurt."

Lex's role as puppet master even has him creating a clone of his dead brother, Julian. "He's never really had anybody in his life," says Rosenbaum. "His mother died at a young age, and so did his brother, so maybe cloning him was the only way he could actually mold Grant into being the brother he always wanted."

Eventually, Lex is sent down a path of darkness that sees him killing both the Julian clone and his own father. "I think deep down, Lex has always thought about killing his father," reflects Rosenbaum. "In season one, when the Luthor mansion caved in, he could have killed him right then — but he didn't. Every year, building up, there were moments when he thought, 'I could take your life right now.' Remember that scene in [season three's] 'Shattered' when Lex went crazy and was getting electrotherapy? Who would do that to their own son? There's every reason for him to kill his father, and he didn't because he was trying to do the right thing," Rosenbaum adds, defending his character's actions. "For all these years, Lex has been trying to stay on the right path and not veer off, and now, finally, I think the key means more to Lex than his father does. He's holding the secret everyone has kept for so many years, andtried to deter him from discovering. I think this is the moment where he has a quest, when he says 'Do you think King Arthur regretted pulling the sword from the stone?' He asks Lionel why he gave up on this quest. The irony is, he's not giving up *his* quest to find out what's at the end of the tunnel."

Above: Lex uses Kara's amnesia to his own advantage.

In the end it is this quest, to find out the truth about Clark, that drives Lex to finally give in to the urge to kill his father. "He's always known Clark was different," Rosenbaum notes. "He's always known that there's something bigger going on than anybody believed that he knew. He had all of these little clues, this cellar full of trinkets, videos, and models, and it all adds up. Just when they think that he's going to let go of all this — when he shuts it all away and locks it up — it comes back."

"By killing Lionel, you push Lex over the final threshold of where he's going — that point of no return," Al Gough explains. "The idea had its seeds in season two, it was something that we were thinking about for season four, and then it finally came to fruition in season seven."

"There was still a last vestige of good in him — the little boy, that little Lex, Alexander, that came to him in 'Fracture' and 'Descent'," adds Turi Meyer. "But he has now exorcised whatever good was left inside him. He's become the Lex Luthor of the mythology: the evil, power-hungry egotist that we know and love." Holly Harold adds, "That's it. You see him kill his inner child, the good side of himself."

Sadly, season seven also marked the end of Lex Luthor's *Smallville* journey, as Michael Rosenbaum's contract with the show ended after seven seasons. "We knew that his contract was up," Kelly Souders says. "We all hoped that he would be back next year. He's a phenomenal actor, and we never gave him a scene that we weren't totally impressed with. But we did know the reality of his contract being up, so when we wrote the finale we wanted to make sure that if for some reason he didn't come back, he didn't just disappear into the ether. We wanted him to have a culminating scene that would hopefully satisfy the quest that he's been on for seven seasons."

Rosenbaum himself is still amazed at the success of his character and the show. "My experience has been a plethora of mixed emotions," he says. "Playing a character of this magnitude has been challenging, rewarding, and it has been everything I've wanted it to be and everything I didn't want it to be... I'll never forget it. I don't think you could forget something like this. Most series last a year, maybe two years, tops. But to be on a network for seven years and still be one of the top-rated shows on that network is extraordinary, as well as the amount of fans. I mean, if it wasn't for *Smallville*, I think everybody would be saying, 'Hey, You look great in drag!'" Rosenbaum laughs.

As he says goodbye to the show that has been the center of his life for seven years, Rosenbaum has nothing but good things to say about his fellow cast and crew. "They're so different, and I respect each one so much," he says as he reminisces. "A lot of times, you hear about egos getting in the way. I remember I looked at Tom when we were doing the pilot, and I went 'Hey, I just want you to know there's no room for ego on this set. Just mine, that's it, I'm the only one that can have an ego.' And we laughed. When I tell a joke, he's the first person who laughs. He's there every day, and it takes a lot. I'll miss moments. We had some great moments where we laughed until we cried, and really enjoyed ourselves. There wasn't a day that went by when we didn't have at least one good laugh. Even with a tough episode, where maybe we didn't like the story or the director, we somehow made light of things and laughed. We're like one big family. I think that's the hardest part," he continues, "we're one big family, and then that's it. You might see a few of them here and there, but you can't see them all like you used to every day, and at the time you take that for granted, I think. Everybody I've worked with is great. John Glover and Annette O'Toole and Schneider were awesome to work with. They're role models; just good people. Allison Mack, always smiling, always going to a museum and telling everybody about how great the museums are, and I'm like 'How many museums are there in Vancouver?' Kristin, cute as a button. We became really close in the last year or two. First person to give me a hug, I see her — hug. First couple of seasons, we didn't like each other. It's so funny how things just turn around," he says with a smile.

Above: President Lex, from the alternate world of the episode 'Apocalypse'.

"I have no plans to come back, but you never know what will happen," Rosenbaum adds. "So, I'll just leave it open and say that I really want to grow my hair out and do comedies. Seven years is a long time for a series. We're very fortunate, but after seven years it's time to say goodbye to my character."

Rosenbaum concludes with a shout out to the much-loved loyal fans of *Smallville* — and a last attempt to defend Lex's evil actions. "I just want to say thanks to everybody that watches *Smallville*. If someone ever says 'I love *Smallville*,' I always take the time to shake their hand or thank them. If I don't see you, remember, Lex wasn't that bad of a guy, he was trying to do the right thing," he laughs. ∎

# LOIS LANE

**"You know, if I didn't know any better, Smallville, I'd think you were worried about me."**

Just as Clark continues on his journey to becoming Superman, Lois Lane is on the path to becoming the ace reporter famous in the comic books, movies, and TV shows of the last seventy years. As early as this season's second episode, Lois moved forward in her career by landing a job at the *Daily Planet*. There, she begins a romantic relationship with her new editor, Grant Gabriel.

"I think Lois saw Grant as a rebound from Oliver Queen," Caroline Dries notes, "and I guess when you've dated Oliver Queen, it's really hard to find a replacement. She saw Grant as this guy to banter with. He's cute, he's charming, and she obviously loves a fight, so he was the perfect candidate for her to date. She liked him with her mind, while he liked her with his heart."

Lois embarking on a relationship with her boss caused some controversy. "That raised a lot of questions," admits Dries, "but I think it was no big deal. Chloe brought up a good point, by saying that it's not like Lois was using him to get assignments."

When Grant Gabriel was gunned down, there was no reaction from Lois on-screen, and many fans wondered if she was being insensitive, or if she just didn't know what had happened. "I don't think she knows," Erica Durance reflects. "I haven't been given any moments for her to be able to play that, so I think she just thinks that he's moved away from town or disappeared. I think it'd just be really terrible if she knew that her boyfriend had been gunned down, didn't make any reference to it, and just goes back and makes out with Oliver Queen." Darren Swimmer speculates that Lois assumes that Grant has left and doesn't care to investigate further. "Lois has figured out how to move on from relationships that end badly, and this is no exception," he says.

Oliver's return to Metropolis inspired a variety of emotions for Lois. "I think she feels everything at once, as often happens with matters of the heart," Durance says. "When you really love someone, you have all of these different feelings. She went from being shocked to being very angry to hurt to bewildered, and then to wanting her questions answered. Her way of doing things means she doesn't sit back and wait, as she gets too impatient. She says she'll wait, but she gets too impatient, so she goes after him. You see that happen often when people are in love. They go, 'I'm not going to do that. I'm not going to call him!' And then they call," she laughs.

When Lois discovers that her ex-boyfriend is the Green Arrow, things seem to begin to fall into place. "That's a big 'wow' moment for her," notes Durance, "and everything suddenly makes sense — all of those times he disappeared. Maybe then, in the back of her mind, she thinks, 'Maybe he really does love me, and this is his other mission.' It isn't because, like all the other men in her life, he just decided to go. I think that it justified some things for her and made her, on the one hand, angry that he didn't tell her, but on the other,

it also made a lot of sense. She actually probably found it somewhat comforting."

"When we brought back Justin, we knew that if we were going to bring him back, we'd at least have Lois find out who the hell he really is," Al Gough notes. "There had to be some sort of character revelation out of that so you get to see Lois react, and then we sort of cribbed a line from *Superman II*, when she tells him she doesn't want to share him with the world."

"Romantically, it's been interesting to see Lois grow," Holly Harold says. "I think the Oliver Queen stuff was really pretty amazing, to have her heartbroken, and then to have the opportunity to be back with him and to say no. That was a really beautiful moment to me. I thought Erica played it really, really well. Obviously, it's a play on the fact that she *will* be able to handle the secret of a double life with Clark someday, but it's interesting to have a woman think she wants that relationship, and then at the end of the day, say, 'Now that I know the truth of it, no, I know that's not what I want.' It's a pretty powerful place to put a woman in, which I thought was great."

Season seven saw Lois becoming more and more like the iconic comic book Lois Lane, and Kelly Souders promises more exploration of that in the next season. "She's been so much fun to have on the show; she just brings a new dynamic. I think it was fun to explore all those aspects of her, because she didn't show up at the start of her time as a reporter. We had to help get her to that point, but she became the good reporter that she ultimately is."

Below: Lois's relationship with Grant Gabriel was controversial among the show's fans.

"I think Erica's really grown as an actress," Todd Slavkin puts in. "She was always good, and now she's great, and her comic timing gets better and better. She and Tom, the way they play off each other, it just gets tighter and tighter. Watching the dailies, she makes us giggle," he adds. "She's the best Lois Lane in history. I go on record as saying that. I hold Erica Durance up to Margot Kidder, and up to Teri Hatcher. She's that good."

Fellow writers Darren Swimmer and Turi Meyer concur. "In the same way that it was a tough role to take for Tom Welling, and he lives up to it in the best manner possible, I think that's becoming true for Erica also," says Swimmer. "She's becoming a Lois Lane for future actors to live up to."

Above: Lois tries to stay one step ahead of Lex Luthor.

Meyer adds, "She's really starting to get her legs as a reporter, and becoming the icon and dedicated reporter that we all know and love."

As the season progresses, Lois becomes more wrapped up in investigating the Luthors. "Lois is onto Lex," Holly Henderson explains. "She knows that more than likely, he killed his own father. She sees him as a bad, bad man, so she is always looking for information on Lex." Some of Lois's investigations have involved her teaming up with Jimmy Olsen, much like she does in the Superman comic books. "It's interesting, because they have a great buddy chemistry on-screen that's fun to watch," Holly Harold says. "It's a play on where we've been in the past with Chloe and Clark, and the fact that they're heading down these trails of clues but not really knowing as they're the innocents. Those are some fun, fun moments."

Eventually, as hinted at in the season finale, Clark might join the Lois and Jimmy team. "Lois has said in the past that she thought Clark would make his mark on the world through journalism," notes Don Whitehead, "and I think Lois has very specific ideas of how Clark should go about that. She's not shy in sharing those things." Lois's hints with a *Daily Planet* application may be the genesis of an iconic and much-awaited pairing... ■

# CHLOE SULLIVAN

## "Clark, you're going to have to fly solo on this one 'cause my dance card's completely full."

This season of *Smallville* premièred with Chloe in a morgue — she had used her meteor ability for the very first time, a healing power that has the dangerous side effect of taking a bit of her life force when she helps someone else. Although Chloe recovers, the revelation of her power and the ramifications of using it are shocking to her.

Chloe's insecurities about her new ability make her consider Dr. Curtis Knox's controversial treatments — even at the cost of her recent memories. "She's not happy being a meteor freak," Al Septien says. "There's a lot of danger in being a meteor freak, and she knows a lot of them eventually go crazy. Even if she doesn't go crazy, having this particular power is a big responsibility for Chloe. It's a threat to her life: she saves Lois and almost dies because of it. It's a burden that she has to carry. It's for that reason and because she doesn't want to have to be a meteor freak that she's willing to go to this extreme," he continues. "She just can't stand it anymore. She sees what having secrets and powers does to a relationship, by virtue of her relationship with Clark and seeing firsthand what he's gone through, and she doesn't want to put Jimmy through that."

Allison Mack agrees that her character's new state put an incredible strain on her relationship with Jimmy. "I think that the relationship was suffering because, all of a sudden, it was like Chloe was getting a taste of what Clark has been going through with Lana for the last six years," she explains. "It's like she can't really be honest with her partner, and it was getting more and more out of control and more and more consuming. She was just pulling further and further away, trying to protect him, but really it felt like she was hurting him."

"Chloe's always felt like an outsider, and this has only pushed her further away from normalcy," Todd Slavkin notes. "She's wrestling with this identity where she knows that she was never the in-girl in high school, and she's certainly not going to be the in-girl in adulthood. She will always have that outside perspective."

The back-and-forth with Jimmy and Chloe has caused some fans to see it as a redux of "Clana" from early seasons. "Chloe and Jimmy aren't romantic enough to be like Clana. We're too goofy," Mack laughs. She also thinks that it's Clark, not Jimmy, who causes Chloe the most problems. "I don't think her relationship with Jimmy holds her back," she says. "I think her relationship with Clark holds her back from her relationship with Jimmy."

As the season progressed, Chloe began to come to terms with being one of the meteor-affected. "She started out not accepting who she was," Al Septien explains. "She wanted to change her life completely so that she could be the image of who she thinks she has to be, and what she realizes throughout the season is that she could accept who she is, and she is who she is. That comes with flaws and meteor infection and everything,

Above: Chloe's hacking skills landed her in serious trouble by season's end.

but by the end of it, she's stronger. She's with a guy she loves, a guy that really loves her. She's the more positive story of the season. It's not tragic; it's actually a very hopeful story. In the whole series, there have been all these meteor freaks that are just suffering through their lives, they're always just waiting for the other shoe to drop. Chloe is a person who realized she was a meteor freak, struggled with it, and then at some point during this season came to terms with it and is actually living her life happily, despite this burden she carries."

During 'Siren', it was revealed that in addition to assisting Clark, she had also been helping Oliver Queen on the side. "I think she's kind of like his right-hand man," Justin Hartley says of the alliance. "She's there, she already knows his identity, and he can trust her, so he really doesn't have to worry about that aspect of it. She's bright, she's brave, and she knows what she's doing. He just tries to do things through her and keep out of trouble."

In the episode itself, Clark accuses Oliver of putting Chloe in danger. "I don't think that Oliver ever intended for something like that to happen," says Hartley. "Maybe it was a little careless, but it worked out all right in the end." Hartley also points out that we never did see Chloe's recruitment on-screen. "You have to imagine what exactly went down in that conversation. The way I played it was that she all but volunteered to do it; I don't think I twisted her arm. She's a grown-up."

"That was fun," Allison Mack says of her chance to play alongside another hero. "I love all the episodes where we do the really serious comic-book super hero stuff, because my character has the opportunity to really play up the sidekick thing."

When Lex buys the *Daily Planet*, suddenly the world's greatest newspaper isn't the best place for Chloe to be. Mack notes, "I think life becomes a lot less private and a lot more dangerous, because all of a sudden someone she is trying to hide everything from has access to it all." In the episode 'Descent', Lex has her fired.

Of Chloe's departure from the newspaper, Holly Harold says, "The *Planet* had always been her dream, but life changes, and so does her dedication to Clark, and I guess what I would call her higher calling." She adds, "Evil is out there. The Lexes and the Brainiacs can and will hurt humanity. One job at the *Daily Planet* is not all that, because she has bigger calling." Caroline Dries adds, "I think she's almost retiring her career and she's going to become a selfless, full-on sidekick of Clark Kent, where she's working toward the greater good."

Allison Mack feels that her character is still a reporter, but her priorities have changed. "It's my opinion that her life is now less about her career as a reporter and more about reporting as a cover and a tool to be the assistant to a super hero," she says.

For a two-week period in May 2008, the producers and fans of the show were in a state of worried uncertainty as a deal had not yet been made for Allison Mack to continue with her role in season eight. Kelly Souders reveals what was worrying the writers at this point. "When it really looked like she was not going to be back," she says, "I think what the four of us [executive producers] were wrestling with the most was the fact that without Chloe, Clark doesn't have his own personal world. Chloe's really the only one on the inside with Clark Kent, so when you take her away, he becomes an island. Although that can be poetic and romantic, when you're watching television and you want scenes to happen that are emotional, it becomes a critical obstacle." Fortunately, a deal was made and Allison Mack was signed up for season eight.

Reflecting on Chloe's future, Todd Slavkin says, "We want her to evolve. I think she'll always have journalism — that's how her curiosity began in terms of her professional career, but that's not all Chloe Sullivan is. In season eight, we'll see a whole other side of Chloe that will amaze people."

Souders concludes that Chloe's alliance with Clark means her life will never be easy. "I think one of the complications of being close to Clark Kent is that it's like being close to the Messiah," she says with a smile. "Everything in your own personal life is going to take a back seat because you're trying to serve Clark Kent, and you're trying to serve the greater good. How are you ever going to look at an article on the latest building going up in Metropolis as more important than helping Clark Kent save people's lives? That's one of the struggles that's interesting for her." ∎

Above: Whether it's in the *Daily Planet* newsroom or inside the Talon loft, Chloe is always a trusted confidante, helper, and friend to Clark.

# KARA ZOR-EL

"Zor-El told me that Krypton's salvation was on Earth, and that you and I were the key. I hope we're not too late."

L iterally flying into *Smallville* for its seventh year after waking from a suspended animation slumber, was Kara, Clark's cousin from the planet Krypton. Chosen to play the role was Laura Vandervoort, a Canadian actress best known for her work on the teen series *Instant Star*.

"I'd met Laura prior to working on the show at Comic-Con in San Diego," Phil Morris remembers. "I found her to be captivating, incredibly beautiful, and just a very winning girl. It's a difficult trek to start out as Supergirl, but if anybody could do it, it was Laura."

Vandervoort was quickly welcomed on the set by her co-stars, and found a kindred spirit in Erica Durance. "Coming in new after seven seasons, I was obviously nervous," Vandervoort recalls. "Erica knew what it was like to be the new girl in town, and she said to me, 'You know, it'll all die down. In the very beginning, it's quite overwhelming, but you'll get used to it.' She was very understanding."

Before hitting the screen, Kara was initially written with a slightly different twist. "When I auditioned, she was more of a Paris Hilton-type character," says Vandervoort. "I wanted to put a little more depth into it and a little more strength, and I think they liked the way I was playing it and worked around that to rewrite it."

Vandervoort's work on the character impressed the show's writers before her first episodes even aired. "When I saw the dailies for Kara, where she was picking up these kids in the playground, I remember laughing so hard," says Caroline Dries. "I thought she did such a great job because she's this beautiful, petite little girl who's this total badass, strong woman. It's like there are two opposing personalities in one girl," she smiles.

"Clark had been alone for a long time," Al Septien notes. "He's had human relationships, but he'd never had anyone that was like him. And then finally, in this season, he's met someone who is like him. It also gave Clark an opportunity to grow up and be more mature, to be the parent in the relationship."

Kara's early stories are fueled by her desire to find her crystal, which she sees as a connection to her life on Krypton. In the episode 'Lara', we see glimpses of that life. "One of the things we love about this show is the fact that we can delve into the DC Comics mythology," Don Whitehead explains. "We enjoyed starting off Kara's back story to reveal why she feels so tied to Zor-El. In 'Lara' we wanted to see that father-daughter moment where she has to leave Krypton and follow her destiny. You can see in both their eyes that there's a lot of love, and that set Kara up for her arc through much of the beginning of the season. She had to find her hip; she had to find that crystal. Her father gave her something to do, and she had to see it through."

Above: Kara as the waitress, Linda (left) and in a more glamorous mode (right).

He adds, "Even at the end of that episode, she talks about how she thought her father was a god — a real Kryptonian hero."

Kara's relationship with her father is further explored when his replicant appears in 'Blue'. "Obviously Zor-El is kind and loving when he first arrives," says Vandervoort, "before we find out the truth about him. He's trying to convince her that his ways are the right ways, but she soon realizes when his anger boils, what type of person he truly is, and, obviously, she has her memories which show her how he treated Lara inappropriately and things like that."

Jimmy is one of the first humans to catch Kara's attention. "Kara hasn't really known many humans before, especially ones so considerate and compassionate," notes Vandervoort. "He was there for her when she needed him, and he doesn't know anything about her powers, so he just accepts her for who she is. She needs someone like that in her life, because the other man in her life was her father, who was very strict and not very emotional or compassionate, but Jimmy was there for her."

Aaron Ashmore adds, "I think that basically what she sees in Jimmy is someone honest and straightforward, and I think she responds to his innocence and his energy. It's something that she sees. When she first comes to Smallville, there's a lot of heavy stuff going on, and I think he's a little bit of a distraction."

After the appearance of the Lara and Zor-El replicants, Kara finds herself in Detroit, and an amnesiac. She works at a diner there, believing herself to be a

woman named Linda. "It gives her a glimpse of what it's like to be a real human being," Vandervoort says. "She gets to have a normal lifestyle, just working at a diner like a young girl, and she has a bit of a romance there. She has a whole new life, but then, when she realizes who she really is, she appreciates the truth even more."

Some of Vandervoort's favorite scenes were when her character got to be physical. "I've always loved the physicality," reveals Vandervoort. "I did martial arts when I was younger, so I found that part to be a highlight, especially when you're acting all day, it's a bit of a change."

At season's end, it is revealed that the real Kara did not return with Clark from the Phantom Zone; the Kara who returned was really Brainiac in disguise. Meanwhile, the real Kara is lost in the Phantom Zone, and Laura Vandervoort has departed the series after only one season.

"We didn't want to repeat the Clark Kent storyline of being an alien and becoming human and asking 'How do I fit in?'" Todd Slavkin adds. "We did a few episodes, which was great because Clark could relive that part of his life and pass on to his cousin the wisdom that he has from going through all that himself, but after a while those stories played themselves out."

Darren Swimmer ponders if there were many more stories to be told with Kara, but he concedes that: "Once she'd come to terms with who she was and what her parameters were on Earth, how much more was there to do?"

Despite her limited run, the show's writers are happy to have had her for season seven. "I thought she was an awesome asset to the season," says Caroline Dries, "and she really fueled a lot of story and gave Clark just one more ball in the air that he had to juggle. She was really fun." ▪

# JIMMY OLSEN

"Is this the point where the sad song comes on and we break up all over again? Because I'm not going to make it that easy this time."

Smallville's seventh season was where Jimmy Olsen truly matured. His relationship with Chloe grew from hurt feelings due to initial secrecy to learning her secret and then almost losing her. He met Clark's cousin Kara and they had a short-lived romance. Jimmy also began to take on his iconic role of pursuing scoops at Lois Lane's side, and on his own he started to learn about Smallville's mysteries, including the Kawatche Caves. Jimmy also found himself in serious trouble when he got involved with a violent DDS agent named Vanessa Weber, as well as being indebted to none other than Lex Luthor.

Although Jimmy first appeared in season six, it was not until this season that he became a series regular in the opening credits. "It felt amazing to get a role and then be asked to come back as a regular," Aaron Ashmore says.

Soon after Jimmy's return to the show in the third episode 'Fierce', Chloe's reluctance to tell Jimmy about her meteor affliction and growing distance led to the end of their relationship shortly after in the episode 'Cure'. "That was one of my favorite scenes I've ever done on the show," Aaron Ashmore notes. "It really worked because there was a lot going on, and I think that it came to a point where they were looking at each other like, 'Who are you? I thought I knew you.' I thought it was a really sad scene."

Jimmy suffered a lot of criticism online when it seemed that the character had a roving eye for Kara. "I don't know if it was necessarily the best way to handle the situation, but I think it was a very normal way to react in that situation," Ashmore says. "Obviously, Chloe has been hiding things from Jimmy, running off, not telling him about the whole meteor power, stuff like that. There's some tension, so when this other beautiful girl shows up and she is showing him some attention, I think that was appealing to Jimmy. I don't think that he was necessarily going to act on it or cheat on Chloe or anything like that, but I definitely think that there was that kind of interest, 'Wow, this gorgeous girl is interested in me.' There were things going on between Jimmy and Chloe that Jimmy was a little confused about, so I think Kara's attention was more of a distraction for him. I don't think that he acted badly, he acted like pretty much every normal guy would do looking at Kara."

Holly Harold thinks that it was right for Jimmy to move on when he did. "Chloe broke up with him and really crushed him, and in the words of my co-workers, 'How long does one wait before seizing an opportunity?' He didn't seek Kara out. Kara obviously cared about him, and I think there were a lot of emotional reasons why Jimmy went for someone who wanted him, as opposed to banging his head against the Chloe wall."

Eventually, during a life-threatening situation inside a *Daily Planet* elevator, Chloe finally tells Jimmy about her meteor affliction. "I think that he's really thankful that she

Luthor

Queen

Teague

Swann

Above: Confusing signals from long-time girlfriend Chloe led Jimmy to be drawn to Smallville's latest arrival, Clark's cousin Kara.

opened up to him about her power, and that cleared up a lot of things," notes Ashmore. "Obviously there are still going to be some secrets, but I think he feels that she's put some trust in him, and he feels really good about that. I think that he always has and always will have strong feelings for Chloe."

Although things continued with Kara for a short time after Chloe revealed her power, Jimmy ultimately ended up getting back with Chloe. By 'Sleeper', they were trying to make their second go at a relationship work, and it is at that time that Jimmy makes a deal with Lex Luthor to keep Chloe from going to prison.

"Jimmy made a really bad call when he made that deal with Lex, but he can be impetuous and sometimes naïve," Holly Harold says. "Because of this he'll have some hard lessons in front of him next year as we follow his career and his relationship with Chloe. But ultimately Jimmy is always going to do the right thing — and he would never spy on his friends. If and when Chloe finds out what happened, I think she'll forgive him, because while his original choice wasn't the best one, it still came from a good place. She'd rather Jimmy stand up for what's right than become Lex's puppet."

"Jimmy loves Chloe, and he'll do whatever it takes to protect her," Don Whitehead explains, "and being a headstrong guy, he asks Lex for a favor without thinking about what Lex might ask for in return. When Lex calls in the favor, Jimmy's not happy about it, but he figures that after this one little white lie, he won't owe Lex anything. So it's a surprise when Lex then tries to force him to start spying on Lois. Although he can be awkward, Jimmy's an honest person with a stronger sense of character than some people think — I think that's one of the reasons Chloe likes him. Not only does the idea of lying

turn Jimmy's stomach, he's also not about to become Lex's lapdog. On the other hand, he's mindful of the precarious position Chloe is in. Thinking someone like Lex will respond to a show of strength, Jimmy politely tries to draw a line in the sand. When Lex responds favorably, Jimmy figures he just dodged a bullet. He's blindsided again when the DDS arrests Chloe." Whitehead continues, "Jimmy often finds himself in difficult situations, and he usually tries to work it out by keeping everyone in mind while attempting to remain honest to himself — so he ends up wrestling with a lot of conflicting emotions in a short amount of time. What's amazing about the way Aaron Ashmore plays Jimmy is that no matter how many emotional shifts Jimmy goes through in a single scene, Aaron makes each one clear and believable."

Before Chloe's arrest, Jimmy almost loses her when Brainiac attacks. The near-loss of Chloe inspires Jimmy to take a surprising action, as Holly Henderson points out. "Seeing Chloe in a coma, he was afraid she was going to die," she says, "and he realizes he doesn't want to live without her, so he proposes."

"When he almost loses her, it has such a strong effect on him," Don Whitehead puts in. "Jimmy is an impetuous kind of guy. He goes with his emotions. He grabs that plastic ring and goes down on one knee and says to her, 'I thought I could just live in the world knowing you were in it. And at the end of the day, no, I want to spend the rest of our time in it together.' That's very true and very honest." ■

# LIONEL LUTHOR

"Lex, I know how strong it is, the attraction of the dark power. But it will destroy you. I can't let you go down that terrible path."

Developed specifically for *Smallville*, Lionel Luthor, as played by John Glover, was one of the show's original creations. For seven years the character wavered between good and evil before falling to his death in the seventh season's sixteenth episode, 'Descent'.

The start of Lionel's final season came a little later for John Glover, who didn't return to the series full-time until 'Action'. "I was doing a most magnificent play called *The Drowsy Chaperone* in New York, and I was having the time of my life," Glover explains. "I played the role of 'the man in the chair,' and it was just magical." *Smallville*'s producers accommodated Glover's schedule by letting him start with the fifth episode, though he did film a short scene for the season première.

Holly Harold sees season seven as the end of a long journey for Lionel. "Lionel had this quest, which in the beginning, with the killing of the Queens and so on, was really not an honorable quest," she notes, "but to have seen this and known this, it's clear that Lionel is a man that power corrupted absolutely. To be presented with Clark Kent, who's the epitome of that absolute power, and to see him only use it for good, has really touched his character. It goes back to the transference [when Clark and Lionel switched bodies in season four], and to have experienced that himself and been a part of that, always affected Lionel. In this past season, it really had become about him wanting to do the honorable thing by Clark, and then ultimately sacrificing himself."

John Glover agrees that his character was acting nobly even to the end. "I have been trying to protect Clark from what is coming, and at some point I realize that Lex is going to cause a great catastrophe," Glover says.

"There's a speech in 'Descent' where he says that he's met many great men, but the most honorable of those has been Clark," Harold adds. "It's pretty spectacular for him to say that, and I think really that relationship has been growing over the last couple of seasons, but maybe more this season. Chloe has a line about the people that Clark has lost in his life have all made a choice. It's tough on Clark, but they're making a choice that's selfless on their parts, and that's been important to show in Lionel's journey. I think it's totally believable that the character does that."

"Lionel reaped what he sowed, but he also redeemed himself by the end," Al Septien says. "He was a fascinating and great character in the series because he turned 180 degrees. He started out as a total bastard that was only out for himself. He was like Lex, but he grew to be more like Clark. He ran the gamut in our series. It was sad to see him go, but there's really nothing else that could've happened. He paid for his sins, but before he died, he was redeemed."

# LIONEL LUTHOR

Above: Clark's abductor Pierce pulls a gun on Lionel.

Glover credits Lionel's interaction with Martha Kent as the reason for his turnaround, and he looked to his own personal friendship with Annette O'Toole for guidance in his performance at the time. "Annette *was* Martha," Glover states. "She's such an incredibly generous person, and the lessons I learned from Annette I tried to put into the lessons that Lionel learned from Martha."

"It was disappointing when Annette left, because the writers then didn't know how to deal with Lionel," Glover laments. "It was like going cold turkey off something addictive; she was just gone, and there was nothing. It was like Lionel's soul mentor left. A lot of the way I've been playing this and trying to get to Clark, it's because I remember Martha and Annette and the way she was."

"The seven years have been terrific," Glover says of his multi-year turn as Lionel. "I feel I have grown as an actor, and I think there was the feeling of security in having this job for seven years. The other actors on this show are all wonderful, and most of the guests have been incredible," Glover continues. "Allison Mack is an amazing talent. She was when she got here, and she's become even better. Annette O'Toole is one of the finest, most generous, wonderful actors I have ever worked with. John Schneider was terrific. When we did fight scenes, he was so generous with me, because he could sense that I was not comfortable with it. He was so warm and loving and generous, helping me to figure it out and to have fun with it. Seeing Tom and Kristin grow as actors has been so, so wonderful to watch. The directors have all been incredibly generous, and you couldn't ask for a better crew. There's a spirit up there in Vancouver that's amazing."

"I hate John Glover," Michael Rosenbaum says with a laugh. "One of the worst human beings I've ever worked with. No, I'm kidding. He's taught me so much, and over the years we've called each other father and son. He's such a talented guy. I learned so much from him as an actor, and I grew from watching him and interacting with him.

"He's also a wonderful human being, with things like raising money and awareness for the Alzheimer's fund," Rosenbaum continues. "He's really the antithesis of Lionel Luthor."

Director Mairzee Almas will remember Glover as a "consummate professional" who always brought his best work to the studio. "He always takes it to that extra area, and always investigates it at extra length and immerses himself that extra bit. He's just so passionate about his craft, and he was just a joy to work with," she says. "We will definitely feel his loss."

Co-star Allison Mack knows that she will cross paths with John Glover again, even though his character has departed the series. "John's been my mentor for seven years,

and is one of the most influential actors that I have ever worked with," Mack shares. "He really took me under his wing and he is continuing to teach me what it means to be an actor, and I'm so grateful for that. I know this isn't the last time I'll work with John."

Ultimately, the show's producers felt that this season saw a well-rounded end to Lionel's story. "I think Lionel's track through this series has been one where you watch him be as evil as he could, and then watch him be as wonderful and nice as he could, and always question his real agenda behind both," says Kelly Souders. "We've toyed with him in so many directions over the course of the series that we wanted his last goodbye to be something that was pure, that the audience — and us watching it — would know, finally, once and for all, he was on the good side. He really was trying to help Clark and trying to be a decent father."

Glover also concludes that ultimately Lionel ended his life as a good man. "Whatever secret that's in that safety deposit box is going to destroy his son, and who knows how many other people in the world will be destroyed," he notes. "Believe it when Lionel says, 'I'm changed now. I'm a different man'. He *is* a different man. He still has the temptations, but he knows the power inside that box can destroy Lex. I feel that Lionel has been saved because he's figured out how to atone for his sins, which was in keeping Clark safe. The story in those final episodes was just stunning." ▪

Above: Although Lionel's devotion to protecting Clark had caused him to turn over a new leaf, he also participated in Clark's abduction.

# LARA

## "I thought I would never see you again. It's — it's like a dream."

For many years, Clark's primary connection to his Kryptonian parents was the disembodied voice of his father, Jor-El, in the Fortress of Solitude. With Zor-El's Kryptonian science, Clark is temporarily reunited with his mother in the episode 'Blue', only two episodes after we first see her in a flashback sequence in 'Lara'. Playing Lara was Helen Slater, most famous for playing Lara's niece, Kara, in the 1984 film *Supergirl*.

Helen Slater recalls how her role on the show came about. "Soon after I had done the Metropolis Celebration, I was sent an article that said they would like to have me come on the show," she says, "and not long after that the producers offered me the role of Lara."

Choosing to do *Smallville* was not a difficult decision for Slater. "I love the show, and I feel the mythology of it is so great," she says. "We knew it would be at least two episodes, and then they killed her off," she laughs. "If anything, I suppose if they want to bring her back, this is the place where they can do it, because it's science fiction."

"I wanted to give that feeling of warmth and love Lara has for her son; I thought that was really important," Slater says about her approach to playing Clark's mother. "I felt that she'd have a peaceful energy as a mother figure to him, and also to counter how Chris Heyerdahl was playing Zor-El. It just felt like that was the right vibe to go for."

Her appearance on *Smallville* allowed Slater the chance to work with Laura Vandervoort as Kara, the role she had played in the classic film. "It was great," Slater recalls. "She's an absolutely beautiful girl, and a very talented actress. I think the only odd part of it when I was working with her was thinking 'Gosh, is that what I was like back then?' It's been over twenty years. I had a special feeling about her and related to her, having played that role myself."

She sees both the pros and the cons when comparing her experience to Vandervoort's. "I got plucked out of obscurity and lived in England and made a big movie, and so it was more momentous; whereas Laura has been working for a few years, and I think in the television world you're a little more protected in general. In terms of her character's arc and how it's been written, I think it's great for an actress to get to play that kind of part, because it's pretty multi-dimensional. This role is probably better than the role in the movie in that she can be more human, because that is what *Smallville* does, it allows these heroes to be very human, and I think that's a really good thing."

Slater really enjoyed the costume that was designed for her character as well. "I loved it. It was like this Greek goddess. I felt very, very Mount Olympus, very beautiful," Slater beams.

"At the start Kara saves Lex in her Kryptonian garb which had a very Roman feel to it," costume designer Caroline Cranstoun explains. "It felt right for Kryptonian clothing to have an ancient mythology feel, so we stuck to something like that for Lara — a more elegant, mature version of Kara's short little Roman costume."

"I had a fantastic time on *Smallville*," Slater concludes. "I felt so taken care of, everyone was so attentive, and it really was just a great working experience." ▪

# GRANT GABRIEL

## "Nothing like a little family rivalry to keep the bullpen hopping."

" I think when I took the role, the description I got was 'new editor at the *Daily Planet*,' and it may have said 'love interest for Lois Lane'," Michael Cassidy says, remembering the casting notices for his character. "It didn't have anything about what would come to be my relationship with the Luthors."

Upon taking the role, Cassidy paid attention at his first costume fitting and noticed how well dressed Grant Gabriel was. "The guy obviously belonged in this situation of running a major newspaper," he notes, "and so what I tried to focus on was that he was somebody who probably had never failed in his life and, as a result, carries himself in a certain way and talks to people a certain way. I'd talk to somebody as though what they had to say or their answer to my question didn't really matter. If you'd never failed in your life, why would you ever slouch? You wouldn't have any reason to. You would always carry yourself really well; you would sort of float around. So that's what my imagination was saying to me, and those were the things that I worked on."

Cassidy particularly enjoyed working with Erica Durance, who shared many scenes with him as Lois and Grant's relationship bloomed into a romance. "Erica is, as an actress, very present. She pays attention to what you do and responds to it, and those are the best kind of actors to work with. It doesn't even matter whether or not they're good — she happens to be good as well, but you don't have to be good — you just have to pay attention, and it's fun to work with people like that. In that way, it was really easy. On a lot of days, it didn't even feel like I was working, because she and I were just goofing off, and then they'd start rolling the cameras and we'd goof off some more, and then they'd cut, and we'd goof off some more, and then we went home. It was just a blast."

Cassidy relished the reaction his character had to Lois, who spun into his well-ordered, successful existence like a whirlwind. "What I enjoyed about that relationship was that it was as though they were wrapped up in something that was beyond their control," he explains. "For Grant, who probably hasn't failed all that much or met too much opposition in his life, meeting a girl who isn't desperately head over heels for him — at least as far as he can tell — and who doesn't really display any interest in him other than getting her story in the paper is refreshing. I found it fun to play a character who is at a pivotal moment in his life."

Despite Lois's initial lack of interest in Grant, their working relationship soon became a romance, which Cassidy feels took his character by surprise. "It's always fun to play somebody who says one thing but feels another," Cassidy notes. "When he snapped at her, and then in the same breath said he'd see her in his office or in the closet in five minutes, it was really about this thing that was grabbing hold of him, and it was possibly the first experience he'd had in his life that wasn't made up or for the benefit of getting somewhere in the professional world. It was really an emotional experience that was bigger than him."

# GRANT GABRIEL

Grant's preference for Lois and lack of interest in the journalistic talents of her cousin Chloe drew the ire of many fans. Michael Cassidy explains Grant's reaction to Chloe: "Grant Gabriel doesn't understand somebody who was at the top of her class, so to speak, in the journalism world in Smallville and then comes to Metropolis and doesn't really do anything," he says. "Chloe does these page five lower-corner kind of stories and doesn't really go after the big headlines. Or, if she did [try hard], it was before he got there, so he wasn't aware of it. Meanwhile, Lois always seemed like she was trying to reel in the big fish. That's what sells newspapers, and that's ultimately what the editor's focus is going to be on."

A whole other side of Grant's character was revealed when it was discovered that he had a connection to the Luthors. "Initially, Grant only finds out that he is related in some way to Lex, and then he finds out that he's Lex's brother," Cassidy recalls. "He actually thinks he *is* Lex's brother, but what is revealed to him, and to us, as the audience, in the course of the first half of the season, is that Grant is, in fact, a clone of the younger brother who passed away: Julian. Lex grabbed some DNA from Julian at some point and cloned a new brother. We find out that he created a couple of different clones, and Grant was the one that worked out."

Below, left: Taking orders from failed Luthor clone Adrian, Lois pulls a gun on Grant.

Below, right: Playing pool with "brother" Lex.

"I think that, for Lex, on a personal level, it's lonely at the top," Cassidy muses of his on-screen brother. "He's got everything in the world he wants, and as a result of that, he's alone all of the time. We see that in our lives; people can't identify with having everything in the world, because most people don't have that. He can have anything he wants, but what he wants is companionship and love and familial relationships, and he can't have that because he's either destroyed them or his wealth and his abilities and everything else have isolated him."

Lex was also using Grant for his position in the press. "In terms of planting his cloned family member at the *Daily Planet*, I think that his motivation was that he's somebody who gets a lot of bad press," explains Cassidy, "and it doesn't hurt to have somebody who controls the press on the inside for you. Also, with any shenanigans that he's working on, if those stories got broken it'd be great to have somebody at one of the most powerful papers in the world putting the cap on those," he laughs.

Cassidy knew his character was in trouble as soon as Grant defied Lex, and sure enough, Gabriel was killed in the episode 'Persona'. "When Lex and I started to argue, or when I told him off, I was like, 'Well, I'm going to get fired. He's going to buy the paper — which he ended up doing — and then he's going to fire me!'" laughs Cassidy. "When I read the episode where I get shot, I was like, 'Well, that's cool. I've never been shot before. This is going to be awesome.' And it was. It was really fun!" ∎

# THE BLACK CANARY

"This is more than just about money, pretty boy. This is about something that you and your merry band of thieves may not understand: Justice."

**W**hen *Smallville* brought back Green Arrow for 'Siren', the show's creators decided to introduce legendary DC Comics heroine Black Canary into the show's mythos. Playing Dinah Lance and her alter ego Black Canary was Alaina Huffman. "The only difference to the usual audition process was that they wouldn't tell me who the character was," Huffman recalls. Though as soon as she was told she was playing such a major character, she knew she had to find out more. "I bought a few of her comic books and did some research online, and I really enjoyed learning about her," Huffman reveals.

To create the distinctive Canary look, costume supervisor Caroline Cranstoun looked to various incarnations of the character from the comic books. "There was the 1940s and 1950s version, which was like a Playboy bunny costume: a curvy, corseted, strapless thing that was not at all action-friendly," Cranstoun laughs. "Another that had a more Lara Croft/ Tank Girl feel to it, and we decided to go in that direction. It was a zipped, sleeveless body suit with a boot that was really flat and practical. It always had little accents of yellow, so we kept that, and we kept the long gloves. She also had a jacket that she wore sometimes. It was fun."

"I thought it was sexy as hell," Huffman recollects of her first impression of Black Canary's crime-fighting uniform. "But then I remembered, comic book characters are drawn, they don't have to go to the gym, so there was a little shock factor there," she says with a smile. "Fortunately, the costume was fitted for me, and I actually felt very comfortable in it."

Black Canary's mask was a key element to the costume. "They did a few tests of the look," Huffman remembers. "Initially, they actually put on a leather mask. In the comic book sometimes she wears the mask and sometimes she doesn't. They decided to go with a mask, which was cool because it was a definite different identity, as opposed to Clark Kent just wearing the glasses." To protect her identity, the Canary's alter ego, Dinah Lance, wears a dark wig — a disguise that even fooled some of Huffman's co-stars. "Almost everybody re-introduced themselves to me," Huffman laughs. "It was so funny."

Even though her character was introduced as a vigilante for hire, Huffman believes that Dinah does what she does for the right reasons. "Obviously she's got a special power or a gift that she feels she can help with, in a vigilante sense," she says. "In the comic books she comes from a crime-fighting family, so I think it's in her blood."

Huffman would be delighted to play the Canary again should the opportunity arise. "I really love her," she enthuses. "I think she's really complex as both Dinah and as Black Canary, and she deserves to be explored. She's a really cool character who hasn't really been 'done'. She's witty and very confident, and she has an air of, 'I'm here, I don't care what you think about me, I'm going to do what I want.'" She would also be open to the idea of seeing her character alongside the others in Oliver's nascent Justice League. "I think that that would be the next logical step," says Huffman, "to see her really develop into a super hero." ∎

# ZOR-EL

**"Oh, we will be together, Lara. If not here today, then one day through my science."**

Zor-El, like his brother Jor-El, was one of Krypton's great scientists. He was Kara's father and Clark's uncle. Despite his intellect, he is greatly affected by his love for his brother's wife, Lara. Christopher Heyerdahl, who played Zor-El, recalls his character's beginnings on *Smallville*. "The farewell scene where the crystal walls are crumbling and I'm sending Kara off to Earth to fulfill her destiny were actually the first scenes that Laura and I shot together," Heyerdahl says. "It shows the essence of their father-daughter relationship, where we were able to express the love that Zor-El has for his daughter; he's not the all-evil, unfeeling character that we get carried away with."

The relationship between Kara and her father is a close one, though a moment on Earth in Kara's flashback shows a very different side of Zor-El that Kara did not often see. "There's an obsessive side to his love for Lara, and Kara comes in on that and sees a side of him I don't think any father wants a daughter to see," Heyerdahl explains. "It's his more basic, instinctive side. As kids, you certainly don't want to acknowledge that your parents have any kind of physical desires, and it's a very vulnerable state for somebody like Zor-El, who has such a strong ego, to be caught in that scenario. We then get to him having to erase Kara's memory, and it shows what he is capable of doing in order to further his own ends."

"Zor-El is a scientist and forward-thinking man," Heyerdahl continues. "In his mind, the choices that he made were for the greater good, and betterment of his people. There were just sacrifices that needed to be made, that he felt were necessary and viable. Like anyone whom we question in history, either at the time or in hindsight, I believe they all felt they were doing the right thing. They probably went to bed and slept very soundly, and I think Zor-El is one of those people. He believed wholeheartedly in what he was doing."

Heyerdahl did not make a conscious effort to play the character as an alien. "I tried make him as mortal or human as anyone that we deal with on a day to day basis; a very smart, intelligent, powerful, and driven man whom we now find on Earth where he has extra powers, which is just going to be something of a tipping point for his ego and his belief in being able to succeed, and in what he can do," he says. "There was this delicious discovery of a feeling of immortality. To portray this I relied on my feelings of when I was a teenager. In our teen years, we all have this feeling of immortality, that we can never die, we can never be hurt; nothing can ever happen to us. I took that and just magnified it into the megalomaniac creation of Zor-El."

Even though the crystal that re-created Zor-El was destroyed, Heyerdahl believes that there could still be a way for his character to come back. "I think it's definitely possible. The great thing about fantasy is that with somebody like Zor-El and his science, who knows how many bits and pieces he's got lying around, how many things he had hidden up his sleeve. I think it could easily happen if the desire was there." ■

# ADDITIONAL CHARACTERS

Anna Galvin played the role of Lex Luthor's assistant **Gina** in five episodes this season. She explains how she got the role. "I read for two roles: the doctor, and the female associate — she didn't have a name at the time. They asked which role I wanted and I went for the associate, as I thought the associate would have a longer lifespan, and could grow and develop with the plot more easily.

"For the first two episodes, I was just called 'Female Associate', and I had very, very little involvement, so it was a lovely gig, but not very artistically satisfying. I was dying for them to develop me," she admits. In her fourth episode, 'Veritas', Galvin noticed a change. "I had an opinion for once, rather than just exposition. By 'Descent', Lex has taken her on as a confidante and she's finally let her guard down, and it's made her unprofessional," Galvin continues. "She doesn't see that she's overstepped her mark because she's let her heart get involved, and once her heart is ruling her head, she makes mistakes."

Don Whitehead recalls the writers' decision to beef up Gina. "In the tradition of Miss Teschmacher [Lex's partner in crime in the *Superman* movies], we wanted a female assistant who is devoted to Lex and willing to go the distance, all in the name of protecting a boss who's actually rather distant and cold. Obviously she has real affection for him and possibly misconstrues his response. As a result, she takes chances that lead to her eventual demise."

"We were playing with the idea of Chloe being there for Clark," Holly Henderson notes, "and then showing the flip side of Gina being that person for Lex. She really believes in Lex."

"I played her a bit like a spanky madam," says Galvin, "someone who clearly had a good education and considers herself an intellectual peer to virtually anyone. She's trying to make it in a man's world. She's one of those women who is constantly dressed up in a suit, hides behind her glasses, probably hasn't had a boyfriend or kissed a man for a very long time, because she's very career-driven and focused and a real A-type personality." Galvin shared most of her scenes with Michael Rosenbaum. "I had been forewarned that he was a real character and that he'd probably tease me a lot," she laughs. "I got a kick out of his sense of humor, so we got along really well. He was a pleasure to work with."

If Gina could have survived, Galvin would happily return to the role. "I didn't have to die, I could have just been paralyzed, and someone could have resuscitated me," she laughs.

For 'Persona', the Kryptonian scientist **Dax-Ur** gave *Smallville*'s writers a chance to build a mythology around the creation of Brainiac. "Dax-Ur is sort of like the Albert Einstein of Krypton," says Don Whitehead, "and he came up with the theory that an Oppenheimer — or Jor-El — actually then built Brainiac from. It's almost like how Einstein created the theory that led to the atom bomb, and he always felt some guilt because he saw where it went. He may not have actually built the atom bomb, but he always felt it was a misuse of his science. We wanted to apply that to the creation of Brainiac, and that's why Dax-Ur felt guilt after he saw where his theories were being taken. That led him to leave Krypton, to go and find atonement, and then finally, when he met the right woman, he decided he could give up that guilt, and move forward in hope and love. I thought Marc McClure did a fantastic job," Whitehead adds. "He brought a certain gentle strength. You could see that he used to be a super hero, and now he's a man who's a little older, a little slower. There's emotion that comes out in his voice when he thinks about how his technology could lead to the destruction of worlds."

Marc McClure, who played Jimmy Olsen in the four Christopher Reeve *Superman* films and 1984's *Supergirl*, played Dax-Ur. The privilege of working with a legend in the Superman universe was not lost on James Marsters. "I almost got in a fight over him," Marsters recalls. "One of the crew was joking about staple gunning him, and I almost went off. I decided it wasn't my battle and I just bit my tongue, but you do not staple Jimmy Olsen! He was such a nice guy; he was really fabulous. His eyes shine with kindness and anger at the same time. He plays on the kindness and doesn't let you know about the anger, but it's right there, and that's a really cool combination. His character was very salt of the earth, a family man, and a man who was pretending to be less than he was so that he could provide for his family. You have that — and then you get me, who, with this grinning face of malevolence, seems to be bent on the destruction of what the audience cares about."

Above: Brainiac attacks Dax-Ur.

"You go on the fan sites and everybody is like, 'Did he die? Did Brainiac kill him?'" smiles Holly Henderson. "The question of if he was killed or not was kind of lingering, and I like how we left it that way. You could assume that he was killed by Brainiac, or maybe he just took his knowledge and Dax-Ur's okay."

The character that most likely killed Dax-Ur for his information, **Brainiac** a.k.a. Milton Fine, was played by James Marsters, making his first appearance on the show since season five. The scheduling of his reappearance worked well for the versatile actor best known for his role as Spike on *Buffy the Vampire Slayer* and its spin-off series *Angel*. "It's funny, because I was in Wales at the time, shooting *Torchwood* for the BBC," explains Marsters, "and I called my manager and said, 'I was thinking I might want to go back on *Smallville*.' My manager then said, 'Oh, James, I forgot to tell you: they called two months ago,'" Marsters laughs. "I had him call them back and see if it was still open."

The chance to work with Marsters was particularly memorable for Laura Vandervoort, a big fan of *Buffy*. "I knew I was going to be starstruck when I met him," Vandervoort says. "When I was younger I sent a letter to the creator of *Buffy* asking to be on it, and then I auditioned for something else for Joss Whedon years later — and he remembered my letter!"

James Marsters has one thing that he would particularly like to see his character do on *Smallville*. "I would like to finally win, but I know that's not going happen. It can't happen! Brainiac wins, Clark dies, and we all go home. That would be terrible. Just think about Spike and Buffy. You can't have him kill Buffy or we're out of a job," he laughs. ▪

# MEET THE CREW

"It's like one big family." — Michael Rosenbaum

### Property Master

**A**leya Naiman is *Smallville*'s property master. Her job includes creating a lot of the smaller items and set decorations you see on the show. One of the most memorable items seen in multiple episodes of season seven was Kara's bracelet. "It's funny," notes Naiman, "because the importance of Kara's bracelet actually came about *after* we had introduced her character. It was never supposed to have a Kryptonian meaning to it. Wardrobe actually had a couple of bracelets as part of her look when she was first seen underwater in that flowing outfit. They had attached the material of the outfit to the bracelets and thought that was a great look. She was shot with those bracelets, and then an insert list showed that we needed to see Kara's bracelet with the House of El symbol on it," Naiman continues. "We ended up calling it 'Kara's Kryptonian bracelet', and had it engraved with the symbol. Soon it became a really important part of the Kryptonian mystery."

As a good portion of the action on *Smallville* takes place inside the offices of a newspaper, many fake newspaper front pages are created by the show's art department and placed by Naiman and her team. "We create the headline pertaining to the story, and then usually the first paragraph is something that makes sense, in case you catch it on an insert," she says. "The rest of it is usually filler text." When a stack of newspapers is seen, often times a double-sided front cover is created as well as inside pages if they are seen on camera.

One of Naiman's favorite creations for this season was the black and gold cylinder used within *Project: Scion* in the episode 'Wrath'. "It was complicated, and they added some stuff after we had designed it," she recalls, "so we had to make it work based on the design, since it was already made. It wasn't originally designed to roll out of a cabinet and break. I was a bit nervous about that one, but it worked out okay." In the

Below: Kara's bracelet was one of season seven's most prominent and important props.

episode, a cabinet door flips open and the cylinder falls from a shelf and rolls across the floor.

Kara's crystal was another *Smallville* prop that had to be broken on camera. "We created the crystal based on our original Clark crystal: the white one that was in the Fortress which he sticks in the console to talk to Jor-El," Naiman explains. "This one was made a little bit smaller, but it was the same basic idea." At the conclusion of 'Blue', the crystal is shattered. "We know it's going to happen, so we made multiple breakaway versions," she notes, "but it is always hard [to see them break] because you know how much hard work and heartache went into it."

Sometimes, set dressing has to be cleared for rights issues. When certain DC Comics-related action figures were seen in the background of 'Action', clearance had to be obtained. "We got permission to show all of the action figures in a group. It was fine as long as we didn't do any close-ups of any in particular," Naiman recalls. "Even though this is a DC Comics show, you still have to get clearance, no matter what, to show anything that's licensed by DC Comics." Eagle-eyed viewers might spot Black Canary — who made her first *Smallville* appearance six episodes later in 'Siren' — as one of the visible toys. A Warrior Angel figure was created for later episodes, as we saw young Alexander playing with a Warrior Angel toy.

For 'Veritas', in addition to creating the props for the flashbacks to 1989, there was also the difficult task of recreating Dr. Swann's wheelchair. "We only saw him from the shadows, but it had to match what we saw in season two's 'Rosetta' and season three's 'Legacy'," Naiman explains. "The original wheelchair was actually Christopher Reeve's own wheelchair, so we had to recreate it and do it justice." Also key to the 'Veritas' storyline were two lockets worn by members of the Veritas group. "Swann's locket was based on a traditional cameo, it's a swan on a beautiful Wedgwood blue gem," Naiman recalls. "The Queen one is based on the Queen family crest. Both of them were completely manufactured, as were the keys that go inside. It was a very difficult build because the locket had to conceal a key, but not be so big that it looked goofy on their necks."

Naiman is very thankful for the crew of people she has working on her team. "The one thing that I always want to get across is that I couldn't do this without my gang," she says with a smile. "They are unbelievable, and this job is so hard. Tim Bartlett, my buyer/build coordinator, Tiara Motem, my other buyer, Mark Black and Justin Bishop, Michael Holm, my truck supervisor, who is always on the truck and supervises all of the

Above, top: A *Daily Planet* prop newspaper used for the episode 'Veritas'.

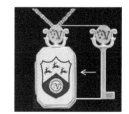

Above, bottom: Designs for one of the Veritas lockets.

props that have to make it to the set. I also have Jared Naiman, who is actually my brother, and he is a man of all trades."

One prop seen in season seven was not a creation of the props department — it was an actual product placement. "We did have to use Stride gum in 'Hero'," explains Naiman, "and we couldn't alter the gum so that it would be seen in a way that it's not actually made."

## Costume Designer

Creating a "bizarre" double for Clark meant creating an opposite look for his genetic duplicate. "Clark was wearing his red jacket and blue T-shirt, so we thought we would put Bizarro Clark in the opposite," costume designer **Caroline Cranstoun** notes. "But it became clear that he needed to look different, too, so he got darker. As it evolved, we realized that black jeans would be better than blue jeans. His jacket was more of a dark blue-gray, and his shirt became more purple. He wore black boots, also, instead of brown boots."

Below: A disheveled look was used for Brainiac's initial return, seen here with Bizarro.

Later in the season, fans sometimes wondered if it was Clark or Bizarro on-screen when the red-and-blue would switch to blue-and-red for some scenes. That was more of a consideration for the sets and the situations that Clark would be seen in. "We try to save the red jacket and the blue T-shirt for the biggest hero moments of the show," Cranstoun reveals.

Soon after introducing Kara to the series, the character got involved in a beauty pageant, which was fun for Cranstoun and her team. "They were really beautiful girls who had great figures, so they all looked fabulous in their bikinis," Cranstoun recalls. "We fitted them all in evening gowns and everybody looked beautiful. We actually did a magician costume for Kara, but that got cut out of the episode."

For 'Action', Cranstoun created movie-style super hero costumes, which had to look distinctive from the ones she created for the Justice League in season six. "That was actually quite challenging, because we wanted to do super hero costumes that would be worthy of a hundred-million dollar movie," she says, "yet would look fake as compared to our super heroes, who are meant to be more 'real'. Certainly with Warrior Angel, he has, I guess, a look that's not as cool: it's more of a leotard, which is a little bit flashy and looks more like a costume."

For Smallville's seventh year, Cranston was also charged with creating looks for two new characters — Grant Gabriel and Kara. "Grant Gabriel was fun to dress," she recalls. "His look was very different from the Luthors — it had a little bit more flair to it than Lex or Lionel had. Grant's look was very well dressed and polished, and he wasn't afraid

Above: The Miss Sweet Corn pageant allowed Caroline Cranstoun's costume team the chance to create several fun designs for Kara and the other contestants.

Above left: Kara's costume with the bare midriff is reminiscent of her current look in the comic books.

Right: Grant Gabriel was given an upscale look even before it was revealed that he was in fact a Luthor.

of color. We used a fair bit of color, and his business suits, if you looked at them up close, had little fine stripes."

For Kara, Cranstoun knew that the producers wanted to go for a bare midriff and shorts. "To try and pull that look together and make it something that worked in action and in fitting with a civilian dress was a bit challenging," Cranstoun reveals. "We went for something that was young looking, that would appeal to young girls, with shorts, a little tube top, and a hoodie."

## Executive Producers

*Smallville*'s creators and showrunners Al Gough and Miles Millar stepped down at the conclusion of season seven, and four long-standing executive producers who have worked on the show since 2002 will be taking their place for the start of season eight. Those four people are **Brian Peterson, Kelly Souders, Todd Slavkin,** and **Darren Swimmer**.

"Al and Miles have worked really closely with us over the course of several years," Brian Peterson says. "They were great at mentoring us and increasing our responsibilities every single year."

"One of the things that we've joked about for years when we're in the writers' room and we're having a brainstorming session, is that we'll say, 'I can hear Miles saying this right now' or 'I can hear Al saying this,'" Kelly Souders says. "Working that closely with them for six years has given us a basis of their vision for the show."

"There's also a sense of always knowing that, when it came down to it, some of the more difficult story or production decisions became 'Well, that's an Al-and-Miles question,'" notes Darren Swimmer. "And we don't have that anymore. The buck stops with us, which is a responsibility that we look forward to having, but they are big shoes to fill."

"The greatest goal for us is to continue the legacy that has been created," Todd Slavkin adds, "and that's a responsibility that none of us takes lightly at all. There are millions of fans out there, and our goal is to please them, and to have them watch every Thursday at eight o'clock and make it worth their while to tune in every week and be as excited as they've been through all these past seven seasons."

"We have had 150 episodes of training, and that's a pretty decent apprenticeship," Peterson laughs. ▪

Clockwise: Brian Peterson, Darren Swimmer, Todd Slavkin, and Kelly Souders.

# THE PHENOMENON

"It's great to have passionate fans." — Al Gough

Seven years and over 150 episodes after it first aired in October 2001, the *Smallville* fan base is still going strong. Fans of the show received their first look at the seventh season at the Comic-Con International in San Diego, California, in mid-July 2007. In addition to a star-studded panel featuring Erica Durance, Laura Vandervoort, Phil Morris, Justin Hartley, and the show's creators, show enthusiasts were also given a video preview of the new season.

Her Comic-Con appearance was Laura Vandervoort's first public brush with the show's large following. "When I first did San Diego Comic-Con, I hadn't shot very much [of the show] and I didn't know what to expect," notes Vandervoort. "I didn't think anyone would actually know who I was or recognize me. But they already knew, and it was nice to meet them. The fans were really, really welcoming."

*Below: Michael Cassidy quickly learned all about Smallville's passionate fan base.*

With the convention also came the announcement that DC Direct would be releasing more *Smallville* action figures for the first time since the show's early days. This time the figures would be based on the nascent Justice League, introduced in season six's 'Justice'. The new toys excited fans and featured accurate likenesses of Tom Welling, Justin Hartley, Alan Ritchson, Kyle Gallner, and Lee Thompson Young.

*Smallville*'s large fan base was something of a new experience for Michael Cassidy, who starred in the series *Hidden Palms* and *The OC* prior to taking the role of Grant Gabriel. He notes that the show's crew were very aware of their relationship with the fans. "It was really fun to work on a show where the crew and the actors had such a deep understanding of their audience," he says. "It's a really cool thing. You go in and immediately you'll hear a grip or a DP saying something like, 'Oh, that'd never fly.' 'Why not?' 'Because they just wouldn't go for that.' And it's not a gripe, it's like the fans really have control, not necessarily over what happens on the show, but they have a voice, and the actors, directors, producers, and the writers especially, are well aware of it and are very respectful of it. That's a level of interactivity that I've never had, even in theatre.

"The producers and the writers read the message boards," Cassidy continues. "They want to know what people think. After my first episode aired, we were already shooting my death because they film months ahead, and Todd Slavkin, who directed that episode, said to me, 'They loved you on the message boards.' And I was like, 'Really?! You read them?' And he's like, 'Oh, yeah, we have to... that's our audience.' That was something that struck me very strongly when I worked on the show."

Allison Mack continued posting on her official website, AllisonMack.com, and making public appearances alongside Kristin Kreuk at *a capella* festivals in New York. She also began developing a new website with Kreuk. Mack explains, "The site will be a place for college students to express and understand themselves, exchange ideas, interact, and have fun." Over on Facebook, Kristin Kreuk and *Smallville*'s unit publicist Kendra Voth launched Girls By Design, a portal for young women to talk and share ideas. Kreuk and Voth frequently post videos on the site and on YouTube to speak to their fans.

Above: Justin Hartley meets with fans.

Allison Mack is very thankful for the large fan base she has and the popularity of her character. "My fans are amazing," she says. "I started my blog about a year ago, and the interactions that I've had with people and the reactions and the feedback and the support and the genuine insight from all of them have just been mind-blowing. I'm so excited, and it's so cool, because I really feel like I've got this whole new group of friends online."

In the offline world, fans traveled across the globe to see their favorite actors at the Grand Slam: Sci-Fi Summit held in April 2008, which featured Aaron Ashmore, Laura Vandervoort, Phil Morris, and Erica Durance. Another treat for fans was Michael Rosenbaum at the Calgary Comic & Entertainment Expo, which he attended only days after shooting his final *Smallville* scenes.

Departing executive producer Al Gough is glad that the fans have stuck with the series for so many years. "It's great to have passionate fans," he says. "You know, sometimes passion can turn against you, but it's always great that people care and aren't indifferent to the show." ▪

# CREATORS DEPART

## "Quite honestly, we got to do what we wanted to do." — Al Gough

In April 2008, as the final episodes of *Smallville*'s seventh season were being shot, series creators Alfred Gough and Miles Millar announced that they were stepping down from their posts as showrunners after the season's final episode, 'Arctic'. Taking their place to run the show would be long-time writer/producers Todd Slavkin, Darren Swimmer, Kelly Souders, and Brian Peterson.

*An open letter from Alfred Gough and Miles Millar, creators and executive producers of* Smallville...

As the creators of *Smallville*, we look back at seven amazing years. We look back at 152 episodes. We look back knowing that the show will continue into season eight without us. After much heartache and debate, we have decided it is time for us to move on.

Over the last seven years we have had the honor of working with a remarkable team of people here in Los Angeles and in Vancouver. We have been blessed with a wonderful cast who we have watched mature with admiration and affection. We have been rewarded with a fan base that is as loyal as it is vocal.

We are incredibly proud of our work on this show. We achieved what we set out to do. We never compromised our vision. We leave knowing that *Smallville* is the longest-running comic book-based series of all-time. The show was featured on the covers of *Rolling Stone*, *MAD Magazine*, *TV Guide*, and *Entertainment Weekly*. The pilot had the highest-rated première in the history of The WB. Even in its seventh year it is still the number one scripted show on the network. *Smallville* is watched by millions of people in hundreds of countries and in dozens of languages around the world.

The show's success is a credit to a fantastically talented group of people. We wanted to take this chance to single some of them out. Our writers — your work speaks for itself. James, Jae, Rob, David — the backbone of our team in Vancouver. Joe Davola, Chris, and Shelly — remember those Friday night brainstorming sessions? Len Goldstein and Steve Pearlman — thanks for believing we could do this. David Nutter — for giving the show your magic touch. John Litvack — when the knives were out, you always had our backs. Ken Horton — our Yoda. Peter Roth — *Smallville*'s biggest fan. Melinda, Michael R., Paul M., Susan and Suzanne — for steering us through 152 episodes. Greg Beeman — your passion is an inspiration. Jordan, David, Garth, Carolyn, Bob & Lew — and everyone at the much-missed WB. Paul Levitz, Greg Noveck, and the guys at DC Comics. Lisa Lewis — our very own soccer mom/accountant. Michael Gendler — aka mega-counsel. David Lubliner — we can finally focus on features now. And last but in no way the least, Renee Kurtz — the smartest TV agent in town, we would be nowhere without you!

Finally, to the fans who have stuck with us through the highs and the lows: know this — we never stopped fighting to make this show great. Thanks for watching.

Alfred Gough & Miles Millar

Gough looks back on some of his favorite moments. "For me, one of the highlights was working with Christopher Reeve. Once we got him on the show it was like a generational passing of the torch from one Superman to the other. I knew then that we were on to something special.

"I love the hundredth episode [season five's 'Reckoning']. That's such a huge milestone for any show, and it gave Jonathan Kent the send-off he deserved. I loved 'Justice' — which could have been a series," Gough laughs.

Another fond memory for Gough was a trip to the Jules Verne Festival in Paris, where *Smallville* was honored. "Going to Paris and having three-thousand French fans singing 'Save Me', that's when you realize the show's had this impact around the world. I remember writing the pilot script with Miles in his apartment, eight years ago this summer."

The original conclusion for *Smallville* as envisioned by Gough and Millar is not known to their successors — and Gough does not feel right sharing that ending at this point, as it may step on the new showrunners' plans. Gough also thinks it's unlikely he and Millar will return to write the series finale. "I doubt it at this point. We have our movie projects, and I think that ship has sailed," he says.

Above: *Smallville* creators Miles Millar and Al Gough.

Gough did confirm that their version of the series finale would include Lex Luthor, and that Chloe would not become Lois Lane in the end, as some fans have postulated. "Chloe, from the inception of the show, was always Lois's cousin," he insists. "It might have even been in the pilot script. The idea that she was going to turn into Lois was never going to happen."

Over the years, *Smallville* has definitely performed — as of this writing, it is about to start its eighth season, even outliving its original TV network, The WB. "Most Superman series had only lasted four seasons," Gough says, recalling the *Lois & Clark* and *Superboy* TV series. "We thought that if we could get to season five, it would be extraordinary. There were times where we weren't sure, especially in this climate of television shows. What series go eight years anymore that aren't crime procedurals?"

It hasn't always been easy, but Gough is pleased they have maintained their standards through the course of the series. "To have had the fans stick by the show and be really passionate was always great," he says. "*Smallville* is a show that people continue to talk about and could get excited about every season, which was always a challenge — to figure out how to shake things up and do something new. Mercifully, we had a great cast and a great staff and the DC toy box to play with as well, which was a great help, being able to take those characters and introduce them through the prism of our show."

Gough looks back at his time as a great experience. "We worked with a lot of great people, and had a great crew. Seven years is like four years of high school and three years of college. If you think about what you went through in that time, it becomes a major part of your life, and becomes family. It's been a great ride, and it will always be a big part of our lives." ∎

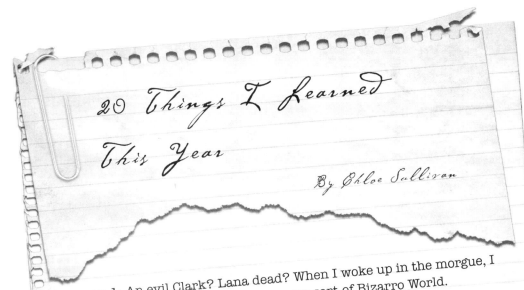

# 20 Things I Learned This Year

### By Chloe Sullivan

Lesson 1: An evil Clark? Lana dead? When I woke up in the morgue, I almost felt as though I woke up in some sort of Bizarro World.

Lesson 2: Kara's arrival gave Clark's life in Smallville new meaning.

Lesson 3: At the Smallville Harvest Festival, competition can get pretty fierce.

Lesson 4: Would a cure be worth forgetting the ones I love?

Lesson 5: Lights and cameras aren't needed for action in Smallville.

Lesson 6: Years after her death, Clark is still touched by the love that Lara left behind.

Lesson 7: Beware the wrath of a superpowered Lana.

Lesson 8: A trap set by a ring of blue kryptonite left Clark faster than a speeding turtle, more powerful than a toy locomotive, and able to leap tall benches in a single bound.

Lesson 9: Lex may have bought the *Daily Planet* to quiet his critics, but the truth about *Project: Gemini* won't stay hidden forever.

Lesson 10: Clark's double's bizarre persona gave off clues that he was not who he claimed to be.

Lesson 11: The thrill of working for Green Arrow pales in comparison to the sound of Black Canary's siren call.

Lesson 12: Clark barely survived a journey into Lex Luthor's fractured mind.

Lesson 13: There comes a time when even Pete Ross can be the hero of the story.

Lesson 14: Patricia Swann wanted to meet with the Traveler; instead, she died far too young.

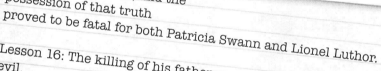

Lesson 15: *Veritas* is the Latin word for truth, and the possession of that truth proved to be fatal for both Patricia Swann and Lionel Luthor.

Lesson 16: The killing of his father was the beginning of Lex's descent into evil.

Lesson 17: Jimmy Olsen, sleeper agent? It could happen.

Lesson 18: Lex Luthor as president with Brainiac on his staff sounds like a one-way ticket toward a nuclear apocalypse.

Lesson 19: Lex's quest to solve the mystery of the Traveler brought the surviving member of Veritas out of hiding.

Lesson 20: When Clark and Lex come face to face in the Arctic, is there any telling what might happen next?

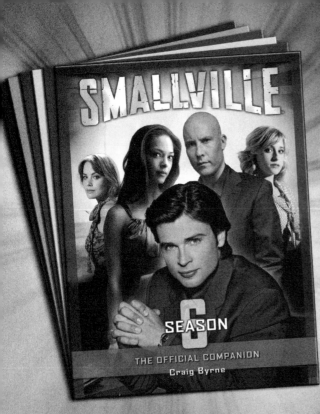